The Restoration of
Cock Robin

The Restoration of Cock Robin

*Nursery Rhymes and Carols Restored to
their Original Meanings*

NORMAN ILES

Illustrations by HARRY ILES

ROBERT HALE · LONDON

© *Norman Iles 1989*
First published in Great Britain 1989

Robert Hale Limited
Clerkenwell House
Clerkenwell Green
London EC1R 0HT

British Library Cataloguing in Publication Data

The restoration of Cock Robin : nursery rhymes and
carols restored to their original meanings
1. Nursery rhymes in English. Anthologies
I. Iles, Norman
398'.8

ISBN 0–7090–3833–X

Set in Garamond by
Derek Doyle & Associates, Mold, Clwyd
Printed in Great Britain by
St Edmundsbury Press, Bury St Edmunds, Suffolk
Bound by WBC Bookbinders Limited

Contents

Acknowledgements

The source-book of many of my quotations is *The Oxford Dictionary of Nursery Rhymes*, edited by Iona and Peter Opie (Oxford University Press, 1951). I acknowledge their care of the nursery rhymes' texts, their notes, and the finding of their tunes.

I acknowledge *The Oxford Book of Carols* (Oxford University Press, 1928), for its tunes, and its words. Also, the Introduction to *The Early English Carols*, by R.L. Greene (Oxford University Press, 1977), for its great help in the struggle between paganism and the Church. 'The Card And Players' from *High Windows* by Philip Larkin. Copright © 1974 by Philip Larkin. Reprinted by permission of Farrar, Straus & Giroux, Inc. and Faber & Faber Ltd.

Nursery Rhymes

Introduction

I have set out to restore the sun. For too long, its gleams have been subdued beneath the clouds of nursery-rhyme nonsense. Resurrected, the rhymes show the basis of our culture, the root of our being.

Together we can rediscover ourselves. You need no special tools to follow my trail. Only an opened eye and a ready smile. The Victorians, with their clumsy camouflage, have successfully thrown the remains of our past into the nursery. There, at mother's knee, misunderstood and misused, we can almost hear the last remnants of the folk truths. Undiscovered, they wait to be lost on the library shelves. Only about fifty of the known recorded rhymes are still familiar today. Without meaning, there is no reason to remember. Soon nursery rhymes may be gone forever.

But the link to the past can be uncovered. It is time to bring the nursery rhymes back from the nursery. The Opies, who made a collection of 550 nursery rhymes for the *Oxford Dictionary of Nursery Rhymes* (ODNR), agree that 'the overwhelming majority were not composed for children'. They are the remnants of 'ballads; folk-songs; ancient

11

and ritual; rude jests; romantic lyrics of a decidedly free nature' (ODNR). Where are these strikingly adult versions? Surely not to be repeated in the presence of collectors – like Cecil Sharp (who went round accompanied by the local vicar). So what happened to the adult sayings, songs and beliefs of the past? They were reduced, with their 'tails cut off, [to being] adopted by the nursery' (ODNR). The folk did not conform to Victorian values, so their cultural heritage was made so meaningless it became infantile.

Today, it's time to Hunt the Wren. She's been dead too long. The evidence for her murder lies before us. It waits only to be examined with unblinkered vision. Our short-sighted materialistic outlook has severed the greatest link with our past – symbolism. Would it really have been worth remembering through rhyme and song that men went into the woods on 25 December to shoot a tiny bird? Yet the hunt dates back to the Druids, and girls today still take the wren as their namesake – Jenny. This is not just a bird of feathers. Once the questioning begins, so perception grows. A rhyme of sexual imagery; now, that *would* be worth a song!

Nursery rhymes are our forgotten store of sexual song. My work is to restore them to their original forms, and to prove my restorations correct. The pieces of our broken past lie before us. My task is to find the sense that makes them whole. I did not need to discover Tutankhamun's tomb. It was lying in front of me. From deduction comes reconstruction. I hope the ODNR has done the textual research for me. Imagery is my tool; and sense is my goal.

The Victorians were careless disguisers. No rhyme can change its meaning without leaving traces of its original purpose. There has to be some clue, some misfit, some jarring of the rhythm. Fortunately, the Victorians were not folk poets. What were the tools of their disguise? Simple, but effective. Changing the sex of the participants is enough to confuse anybody. 'Three *Maids* in a Tub' in the 1798 version of 'Rub-A-Dub-Dub' becomes 'Three *Men* in a Tub' in the 1825 version. Those same Victorians who chopped the sex off African sculptures castrated the 'Old Man' (p. 111). The young men could no longer be initiated to their sex. 'He' and

12

'she' take only one stroke of the pen. But it takes a stroke of imagination to regenerate them.

'Little' is another mind-blocker. It is a term of endearment, familiarity, not an age barrier. The 'little' girl of 'seven years old' who went to Darlington was old enough to make merry work in the woods ('The Little Coat', p. 44). She didn't do it alone, either! Billy 'Boy' was boisterous enough to go off courting a 'lady gay' ('Billy Boy', p. 65). And his gay lady was old enough to be his wife, although she's 'just come from her mammy'.

Already, the question marks have begun to dot our page. Let us look a little further. When a husband refers to his wife as 'my *old* woman', does it mean they don't love each other? 'Old' is like 'little'. It throws a veneer of innocence by excluding the possibility of any sexual goings-on. His 'Old Man' sits between his legs. He's waiting to rise up – as he will in 'Goosey, Goosey Gander' ('Goosey, Goosey Gander' and 'Little Jenny Baker', p. 32). Thank goodness 'old Jack' can manage a gallop down in the ditch ('Down in the Ditch', p. 83). We'd be lost without him.

Finding words that rhyme is fairly easy. Finding rhyming words that combine sense and symbolism takes a poet! A jolt in the rhythm, a jangling rhyme, shows up the censor's pen. In 'Hill Billy Boy' (p. 69) how can 'chair' rhyme with 'ear'? But 'hair' and 'chair' go together; and a special sort of hair does have wrinkles in it! Wrinkly hair and a girl who 'can do most anything' ('Hill-Billy Boy', p. 68) … That's more like it!

Sometimes the censor was too late. A different version may already have been recorded, with parts still intact. By seeing what the versions contain, I can reconstruct the past. In 'An Acre of Land' (p. 18) the different versions give us a choice of acres. Was it my father who left me three acres of land, as in the 1853 version, or my mother who left me one (1901)? There is but one acre left by a mother to her daughter, and that needs a ram's horn to find fulfilment! So the harvest is reaped, and the rhyme lives again. 'Mary, Mary, Quite Contrary' (p. 26) could be the Victorian Mary of 1788 whose garden could grow only pretty maids all in a row, but in the

1780 version she's a 'Mrs Mary' and certainly experienced enough; her verse ends: 'Sing cuckolds all in a row.' She is the lost woman the Victorians would rather not flaunt.

It is this comparison of versions, of missing symbols, that leads us to the rhyme's true meaning. 'Maybe Tuesday' (p. 36) has us counting the days of the week. We can choose between a wedding on a Sunday, a Monday or a Tuesday. Why should it matter which day a girl chooses to be married on? Because our respectable forefathers wanted to make one thing clear – no rolling over in the clover before the wedding day. They were in such a hurry they even tried to get her married on a Sunday.

'Down in the Ditch' (p. 83) would have been nonsense forever without the help of its other versions. From them we know there was once a baby, a trusty sword and our friend, good Old Jack (p. 83). Now we can make merry work and set Jack a-galloping. The addition of 'Tumble-Down-Dick' and a ditch in the 1849 and 1950 versions of 'This is the Way the Ladies Ride' (p. 85) helps us on our journey to understanding. From an amble to a gallop to a jump. From a hedge to a slippery place to a ditch. To tumble-down Dick. We're getting somewhere, fast. This is a sexual ride if ever there was one.

Sometimes unlocking the door into Rhymeland takes us as far as Europe. Lina Eckenstein, in her comparative study of nursery rhymes, agrees. She says: 'In many cases rhymes, that seem senseless taken by themselves, acquire a definite meaning when taken in conjunction with their foreign parallels' (ODNR). She goes on to say: 'Often the same thought is expressed in the same form of verse.' It is from the German folk-version of 'White Bird Featherless' (p. 51) that we know where the bird is flying – straight home to his wife. 'Hunting the Wren' was a custom not only in Britain but also in France and Scandinavia. It was still taking place in Ireland as recently as 1946.

There is a common bond among the nursery rhymes, a bond that binds us all together. All the old proverbs, jokes and sayings of the past have a symbolic power. As C.M. Bowra says in his book *Primitive Song* (p. 272): 'In languages which lack abstractions, imagery takes their place.' Our literal minds have overlooked the basics. Even today we remember enough to know that 'Make hay while the sun shines' has more to it than starting up the tractor. 'When the boat comes in' is not just a nautical event. The imagery and symbols of our past have been suppressed. It is time to bridge the culture gap.

I have set out to re-awaken the forgotten symbols in the nursery rhymes. To do so, I have rejected nonsense. How can birds build churches? Yet, taken literally, that's just what happens in 'The Little Coat' (p. 44). It is time to raise your eyes. Who sits upon the steeples of all the ancient churches in the land? Even we might begin to wonder if we saw a rabbit sitting in his place! From time immemorial, birds have represented their human counterparts. Here, in the rhymes, we can rediscover the bird imagery of the folk. 'What's sauce for the goose is sauce for the gander' ('Goosey, Goosey, Gander' and 'Little Jenny Baker', p. 32). Goose and gander are the birds for woman and man. Seen like this, they can waft us across the water to our wedding day ('The Wedding Wish', p. 80). The robin, with his red breast, has long been the husband of the wren, with her little round nest ('The Hunting of the Wren', p. 73). Bullfinches, peacocks' feathers, gooses' quills, even a bird without a tail – they all have their place in the nursery rhymes.

Animals are man's favourite symbols. The Black Bull is such a strong totem you can still find him when you go down the pub today. Horses – and the words associated with them, riding and galloping – have long had sexual potency ('Ride a Cock Horse', p. 94). Once the mind is linked in to the language of symbolism, so the imagery fits. A girl's 'garden' is the right place to sow seeds. And what of the flowers and plants that grow in the garden? Even now, the language of flowers is the language of love. We still send red roses to our sweethearts. Holly, with his *red* berries and a prickle, has been male ever since ivy first clung to him. And what of the gardener? He's to be found, triumphant, in 'The Gardener and I' (p. 40).

So, finally, we have found our purpose. The nursery

rhymes are our human history, told as no historian ever could. From them, we can reveal a folk wisdom that goes back to the Vikings and beyond. For the Vikings were not merely bloodthirsty plunderers; they actually settled and made their homes here. Many of our rhymes, like 'Hunting the Wren' and 'White Bird Featherless' have Scandinavian equivalents (ODNR). Halliwell points out that the rhymes have been 'sung in the Northern countries for centuries' (ODNR). So we can find in the rhymes a folk-culture whose roots go back to the Vikings but whose themes are current today.

The nursery rhymes contain the story of our suppressed past, our suppressed present. They are what the Christians tried so hard to subdue. Sexual suppression is part of intellectual suppression. A passive, pliable populace is easier to mould into our capitalistic society. Salman Rushdie described my task: 'A poet's work,' he said, 'is ... to name the unnameable, to point at frauds, to take sides, start arguments, shape the world and stop it from going to sleep' (*The Satanic Verses*). The rhymes are awake. They are ready for the celebration of song.

Courtship Rhymes

An Acre of Land
No. 158, ODNR

My father left me three acres of land,
Sing ivy, sing ivy;
My father left me three acres of land,
Sing holly, go whistle and ivy!

I ploughed it with a ram's horn,
Sing ivy, sing ivy;
And sowed it all over with one peppercorn,
Sing holly, go whistle and ivy!

*[The next two verses follow this pattern. Their first and third
lines are:]*

I harrowed it with a bramble bush ...
And reaped it with my little penknife ...

I got the mice to carry it to the barn ...
And thrashed it with a goose's quill ...

[The last verse, however, is:]

I got the cat to carry it to the mill,
Sing ivy, sing ivy;
The miller he swore he would have her paw,
And the cat she swore she would scratch his face,
Sing holly, go whistle and ivy!

(1853)

OTHER VERSIONS
Sing green bush, holly and ivy

(1853)

My mother she gave me an acre of land

(1901)

I have an aiker of good ley-land,
Which lyeth low by yon sea-strand.
For thou must eare it with thy horn,
So thou must sow it with thy corn.

> (1670. This is the beginning of the reply of the young
> woman to 'The Elfin Knight' in that ballad.)

I sowed it with two peppercorns

> (1908. Folk-song collection)

See also the text of the next restoration, 'A Cambric Shirt'.

The nursery rhyme is described as a 'light-hearted nursery,
nonsense song' by the ODNR. Of course, if it is not
understood, it may be considered light-hearted and juvenile.
But it was a folk-song, still sung by adults in the early years of
this century. It shows the direct connection between nursery
rhymes, so often with tunes, and folk songs.

The sources show how the song has lost its meaning. First,
it has become confused, or been made confused, by muddling
the sex of the singer and the number of the acres of land.
Versions offer 'mother' for 'father' and 'one' acre for 'three'.

This 'I' ploughs, sows, harrows, reaps and thrashes. All
these are male symbolic actions. Who else can plough with a
ram's horn? Also, I heard the 'acre' metaphor when I was a
lad. It depends on the pun 'ache-er'. A lad has three acres. A
girl has but one. Therefore it's a man who is singing this song,
about a girl who has one acre of land which her mother left
her. The 1670 source not only confirms this but tells us where
it lies, so bettering the needless repetition of our standard
text.

We have a clear theme. The girl's acre is to be husbanded.
Study of the form of the verses, and collation of sources, will
help us to get the details right. First, each verse should have
two meaningful lines; and – judging by the other versions –
they should rhyme. We have verse 1. Verse 2 needs the 'two'
peppercorns of the 1908 folk-song. Three is the male sexual
number, so 'two' peppercorns plus 'one' ram's horn is
correct. Verse 3 shows its defectiveness by its lack of rhyme,

and its babyish 'little pen-knife'. A better reaping tool is offered in 'A Cambric Shirt', the next restoration. Verse 4 is also deficient in rhyme and sense. Again, 'A Cambric Shirt' offers 'a peacock's feather' instead of 'a goose's quill'.

The last verse is more difficult. There are no other versions to consider. The form shows that here has been the greatest breaking of sense. Two verses have been forced into one. The three lines must be the survivors of four. We have to compose the line that has been lost.

The sense of it is clear. The man has been a 'true lover' of the girl. Now, this 'cat' swears she will scratch someone's face. Common-sense dictates that it will be the man's face this puss will threaten to scratch. So the 'miller' is but another personification of the man, the 'I', who has been the seed-sower throughout the song and cannot now have his place taken by some latecomer. The significance of the 'mill' is that that is where the harvest is ground. The miller does the grinding.

The chorus lines have been trying to help us all through the song! 'Sing ivy … Sing holly, go whistle and ivy … Sing green bush, holly and ivy.' These are not light-hearted, nonsense lines either, for holly and ivy are the pair of evergreens that symbolize man and woman (as in the well known carol 'The Holly and the Ivy', which was an old pagan song before it was converted). It's the way of growth of these two trees that forms the basis of the symbolism. The holly, with red berries and prickles, fits man; the ivy, smooth and clinging, suggests woman – 'Just like the ivy, I'll cling to you.' So the chorus has been telling us – if we will but understand – that the song is about man and woman, and about 'green bush' – and youthfulness, about spring, when 'the sap is rising'.

So a folk-song is returned to the folk. The music can be found in *English Country Folk Songs*, edited by Cecil Sharp, (Novello & Co, reprinted 1961).

21

An Acre of Land

(Restored)

Her mother left her an acre of land,
Sing green bush, holly and ivy;
Which lay low by yon sea-strand,
Sing green bush, holly and ivy.

I ploughed it with my ram's curved horn,
Sing green bush, holly and ivy;
And sowed it with my peppercorns,
Sing green bush, holly and ivy.

I harrowed it with my bramble-prickle,
Sing green bush, holly and ivy;
And reaped it with my leather sickle,
Sing green bush, holly and ivy.

I set my mouse the harvest to gather,
Sing green bush, holly and ivy;
And thrashed it with my peacock-feather,
Sing green bush, holly and ivy.

I set that cat to cart to the mill
Sing green bush, holly and ivy;
And there I swore I'd grind her tail,
Sing green bush, holly and ivy.

And there I gave her all my grist,
Sing green bush, holly and ivy;
And the cat swore she'd scratch my face!
Sing green bush, holly and ivy.

A Cambric Shirt
No. 86, ODNR

Can you make me a cambric shirt,
Parsley, sage, rosemary, and thyme,
Without any seam or needlework?
And you shall be a true lover of mine.

Can you wash it in yonder well,
Parsley, sage, rosemary, and thyme,
Where never sprung water, nor rain ever fell?
And you shall be a true lover of mine.

Can you dry it on yonder thorn,
Parsley, sage, rosemary, and thyme,
Which never bore blossom since Adam was born?
And you shall be a true lover of mine.

Now you've asked me questions three,
Parsley, sage, rosemary, and thyme,
I hope you'll answer as many for me,
And you shall be a true lover of mine.

Can you find me an acre of land,
Parsley, sage, rosemary, and thyme,
Between the salt water and the sea sand?
And you shall be a true lover of mine.

Can you plough it with a ram's horn,
Parsley, sage, rosemary, and thyme,
And sow it all over with one peppercorn?
And you shall be a true lover of mine.

Can you reap it with a sickle of leather,
Parsley, sage, rosemary, and thyme,
And bind it up with a peacock's feather?
And you shall be a true lover of mine.

When you have done and finished your work,
Parsley, sage, rosemary, and thyme,
Then come to me for your cambric shirt,
And you shall be a true lover of mine.

(1784)

OTHER VERSIONS:
At the bed's foot there grows a thorn:
Which ever blows blossom, since he was born:
('Down in Yon Forest', *Oxford Book of Carols*)

A tale in the fourteenth century *Gesta Romanorum* has the same metaphorical story, which may be linked with older Oriental stories. In Germany, it was a folk-tale, recorded by the Grimms.
Cambric is a very fine white linen.

'It may be that the problems in the present version of the song are not impossible of solution: a shirt without seam might be a cobweb; a well where rain never fell, a dew-pond' (ODNR). Of course, it would have to be a big cobweb, and a desert dew-pond. As all the problems are an examination of someone's fitness to be a 'true lover of mine', I thought they might have something to do with love.
Let them make a phallic shirt and a woman's well, big enough to take in a cambric shirt.

A Cambric Shirt

(Restored)

Man: Can you make me a cambric shirt,
Parsley, sage, rosemary and thyme,
Without any seam or needlework?
And you shall be a true lover of mine.

Can you wash it in yon ferny well,
Parsley, sage, rosemary and thyme,
Where never sprung water, nor rain ever fell?
And you shall be a true lover of mine.

24

Can you dry it on yon rosy thorn,
Parsley, sage, rosemary and thyme,
Which ever bore blossom since Adam was born?
And you shall be a true lover of mine.

Woman: Now that you've asked me questions three,
Parsley, sage, rosemary and thyme,
I pray you'll answer as many for me,
And I shall be a true lover of thine.

Can you find me an acre of land,
Parsley, sage, rosemary and thyme,
Between the salt water and the sea strand?
And I shall be a true lover of thine.

Can you plough it with a ram's horn,
Parsley, sage, rosemary and thyme,
And sow it all over with two peppercorns?
And I shall be a true lover of thine.

Can you reap it with sickle-leather,
Parsley, sage, rosemary and thyme,
And bind it up with a peacock's proud feather?
And I shall be a true lover of thine.

When you have done and finished your work,
Parsley, sage, rosemary and thyme,
Then I'll have made you your cambric shirt,
And I shall be a true lover of thine.

As cambric is now out of fashion, some singers may prefer a silken shirt. The singer in me does. But not the traditionalist.

'Parsley, sage, rosemary and thyme', are men's as well as women's symbols.

Mary, Mary, Quite Contrary
No. 342, ODNR

Mary, Mary, quite contrary,
How does your garden grow?
With silver bells and cockle shells,
And pretty maids all in a row.

(1788?)

OTHER VERSIONS:
Mrs Mary, quite contrary,
How does your garden grow?
With silver bells and cockle shells:
Sing cuckolds all on a row.

(1780)

An illustration of this text shows a group of men each with two horns growing from his head.

Not for Mary, Queen of Scots! And not for a garden set in Our Lady's convent!

Why ask Mary that question? What is the point of the answer? Both depend on 'contrary'. Obstinate, quite obstinate Mary, how does your garden grow? Why ask this self-willed one? Because she is the type of girl who always says 'No'. Her 'garden' – with such odd flowers in – is the garden of love.

We are, as always, in the world of symbolism, not the world of gardening hints. A folk-song, 'The Seeds of Love', uses the same image:

My garden is overrun,
No flowers in it grew,
For the beds that were once covered with sweet thyme,
They are overrun with rue.

'Thyme' is a pun on 'time', and 'rue' on 'sorrow'. How will a girl's garden of love grow, if she always says 'No'?

I think it will not bear any fertility symbols but be like the garden of the girl in the folk-song. 'Cockle shells', because of the pun on 'cockle', are boy babies; 'silver bells' are girl babies. But contrary Mary cannot have those flowers in her garden. So there must have been censorship, or forgetting, here. Another Mary, a contrasting one, must have borne them. The second verse, which told of her, has been lost, i.e. suppressed. This 'quite willing' Mary had the verse which ended 'Sing cuckolds all on a row.' Contrary Mary could never have grown the extra horn on their heads. She has no cuckoo-spit in her garden. The 'Mrs Mary' of the 1780 version makes her sound more experienced too.

So I have to reconstruct. For the first verse, I have the first two lines, and the life-knowledge that all her flowers will be flagging, unprecious ones (the opposite of 'silver bells and cockle shells'). For the second Mary – the lost girl – I have the last two lines, and the knowledge of her nature.

When I did reconstruct, I also revised. I didn't like the historically correct 'Sing cuckolds all on [in] a row.'

Mary, Mary, Quite Contrary

(Restored)

Mary, Mary, quite contrary,
How does your garden grow?
With matted weeds and tangled reeds
And Ragged Robins ranged in a row!

Mary, Mary, not so chary,
How does your garden grow?
With silver bells and cockle shells
And Wake Robins stood in a row!

The Cuckoo-pint is the Wake Robin or Lords-and-Ladies. (*Chambers English Dictionary*)

Dick-ery, Dick-ery, Dare
No. 131, ODNR

Dickery, dickery, dare,
The pig flew up in the air;
The man in brown soon brought him down,
Dickery, dickery, dare.

(1844)

Can I give you some key phrases? First, what is 'up in the air'? Second, who is 'The man in brown'? The third, 'brought him down'? And the fourth, 'Dickery, dickery, dare'?

It's only letting the mind change the symbols: 'the pig' is the phallus, and 'the man' becomes the girl. Then you'll see why my title becomes 'Dick-ery, Dick-ery, Dare'. You can, at last, get 'dare' too.

It's the simplest of all the rhymes. And, almost, you get it for love.

The rhyme, in ODNR, has no notes about what it means.

Dick-ery, Dick-ery, Dare
(Restored)

Dick-ery, dick-ery, dare,
The cock flew up in the air,
The girl in brown soon brought him down,
Dick-ery, dick-ery, dare.

The North Wind Doth Blow
No. 533, ODNR

The north wind doth blow,
And we shall have snow,
And what will poor robin do then?
Poor thing.

He'll sit in a barn,
And keep himself warm,
And hide his head under his wing.
Poor thing.

(1805)

At Brill
No. 78, ODNR

At Brill on the hill
The wind blows shrill,
The cook no meat can dress;
At Stow-on-the-Wold
The wind blows cold,
I know no more than this.

(1844)

What have they done with our men's poor Robin?
They have neglected 'our'. They have substituted the poor
red-breast to go back in the rhymes. Robin has, no more, a
manliness.

But, wait! Let us put our own poor Robins in. It's cold
enough to freeze the wherewithals off a brass Robin. Poor
thing!

All we have done is changed the tone. The words can stay

nearly the same. Robin still has to hide his head under his wing. But, 'Tain't what you say,/It's the way that you say it' ...

At Brill, on the hill, they still use 'meat' to mean Robin, or Willie, or Dick. There, they they use 'dress' to mean 'stand upright'. The wind does not blow 'shrill' there, but 'chill'. For at Stow on the Wold it blows cold; and Brill must have the same shrivelling wind. When the North Wind blows, Robin hides his head; the meat can't be presented. 'I know no more than this.' But it's enough knowledge to restore both the rhymes.

The North Wind Doth Blow
(Restored)

The north wind doth blow,
And we shall have snow,
And what will poor Robin do then,
Poor thing?
He'll perch in a barn,
To keep himself warm,
Then hide his head under his wing,
Poor thing!

At Brill
(Restored)

At Brill on the Hill
The wind blows chill,
The cook no meat can dress.
At Stow-on-the-Wold
The wind blows cold,
The meat grows less and less.

(B)Randy Hill
No. 77, ODNR

As I went up the Brandy hill,
I met my father with good will;
He had jewels, he had rings,
He had many pretty things;
He'd a cat with nine tails,
He'd a hammer wanting nails.
Up Jock!
Down Tom!
Blow the bellows, old man.

(1820)

I've changed the name of the hill. 'Brandy Hill' would surely have something to do with drink. What this hill has to do with is the 'pretty things' of the father – the family jewels, rings, something with (or without) a tail, a hammer. As these symbols are followed by 'Up Jock! Down Tom! Blow the bellows, old man', we are told that the father's male attributes are about to be used. For the son is doing as his father did before him, on the rise of Randy Hill. Hence the music hall's joviality – 'How's your father?'
All are without comment in the ODNR.

Randy Hill
(Restored)

As I was going up Randy Hill
I met my father with good will.
He had jewels, he had rings,
He had many pretty things.
He'd a bird without a tail;
He'd a hammer without a nail.
Up Tom! Out Tam!
Blow the bellows, my Old Man!

Goosey, Goosey Gander
and Little Jenny Baker
Nos. 190 and 191, ODNR

Goosey, goosey gander,
Whither shall I wander?
Upstairs and downstairs
And in my lady's chamber.
There I met an old man
Who would not say his prayers.
I took him by his left leg
And threw him down the stairs.

(1784)

OTHER VERSIONS:
Old father Long-Legs
Can't say his prayers;
Take him by the left leg,
And throw him down the stairs.
And when he's at the bottom,
Before he long has lain,
Take him by the right leg,
And throw him up again.

(1780)

Goosey, goosey gander,
Who stands yonder?
Little Jenny Baker;
Take her up and shake her.

Giddy, Gaddy Gander,
Who stands yonder?
Little Bessie Baker,
Pick her up and shake her,
Give her a bit of bread and cheese
And throw her over the water.

(1883)

Let's start off right. Let's start off sexually. For 'Goosey, goosey gander' is telling us to. Goose and gander are the birds for woman and man. They are also called on in 'Wedding Wish': 'Gray goose and gander/Waft your wings together.'

They tell us that the wandering upstairs and downstairs, and then into my lady's chamber, has sexual purpose. 'I' am being led on.

In my wife's – or girlfriend's – bedroom, who do I meet? An old man. Not a real old man, a personification. 'My old man' is another way of saying 'my cock'. 'Cock' is from the look of a crowing cock, but 'my old man' is from a very old way of looking at life. It's from the respect for the family, going on and on, from father to father, that is called ancestor-worship when the Chinese and Japanese do it. We still keep the same attitude – though some of the reverence has gone – deep down in our minds. I saw 'You hold the future in your hands' written up in a men's toilet.

My old man will not, or cannot, 'say his prayers'. This is not religious verse. It is sexual verse. So it means my cock will not, or cannot, do his duty. There is only one prayer this single-minded old man can say. It is a prayer the ancestors want to hear.

Frustration leads to violence – much more violence than the forgetting of any real prayers would lead to. The old man is thrown down the stairs, and then,

> Before he long has lain
> Take him by the right leg
> And throw him up again.

Throw him down, throw him up. He has to mount, to 'get up them stairs', to do his duty, to say his 'Our Father'. He won't get much rest till he does.

The other version calls the old man 'Old Father Long Legs', and so confirms our understanding of him. For, as well as the left leg and right leg by which he is thrown, he has one more long leg. The middle one. He is like the crest of the Isle of Man, for that was how our ancestors pictured the island of masculinity. A pub in Liverpool with the three-legged sign is called 'The Legs of Man'.

Maybe the crane-fly, Daddy Long Legs, was once a symbol for man. Maybe, once, it was a totem insect, as the robin was a totem bird. The school-children who say the rhyme to it (ODNR) must be keeping up that old symbolism. No real crane-fly can be hurled up and down stairs by any of its legs. No real childishness will explain this rhyme.

Nor the next. This giddy gander gads about. He's a rover. Little Jenny Baker is to be taken up and shaken by some rover the way a gander shakes a goose. Then she'll have a bun in the oven! For that's what that daft 'bread and cheese' is hiding. A baker needs to bake.

When she's thrown over the water, she'll cross the one-strand river of virginity, as the girl in 'Wedding Wish' does. But this is going to be a rougher passage.

If we put this rhyme with the succeeding ones, Jenny Baker is the wife of the man who had the 'wheelbarrow'. It broke. His old man wouldn't say his prayers. But he mended it, took her up and shook her, threw the wheelbarrow up again, delved and dug her garden, and she found herself on the other side of the stream with a bun in the oven! This way of thinking branches out like a Hindu carving sprouting arms! But its trunk is the union of goose and gander. Hindu gods have their goddesses.

Goosey, Goosey Gander

(Restored)

Goosey, goosey gander,
Whither did I wander?
Upstairs and downstairs
And in my lady's chamber.
There I found an old man
Who could not say his prayers,
I took him by the left ham
And threw him down the stairs.

Goosey, goosey gander,
Whither did I wander?
Upstairs and downstairs

And in my lady's chamber.
There I found an old man,
Before he long had lain,
I took him by the right ham
And threw him up again.

Little Jenny Baker

(Restored)

'Goosey, goosey gander,
Who stands yonder?'
'Little Jenny Baker.'
'Pick her up, and shake her,
Lie her down, and make her,
Seed her cake, and take her.'

Maybe Tuesday
No. 464, ODNR

On Saturday night shall be my care
To powder my locks and curl my hair;
On Sunday morning my love will come in,
When he will marry me with a gold ring.

(1805)

OTHER VERSIONS:

As I was a-walking one morning in the spring,
To hear the birds whistle and the nightingale sing,
I heard a fine damsel, so sweetly sung she,
Saying, 'I will be married on a Tuesday morning.'

I stepped up to her and thus I did say,
'Pray tell me your age and where you belong.'
'I belong to the sign of the Bonny Blue Bell,
My age is sixteen, and you know very well.'

'Sixteen, pretty maid, you are young to be married.
I leave you the other four years to be tarry.'
'You speak like a man without any skill,
Four years I've been single against my own will.'

On Monday night when I goes there
To powder my locks, and to curdle my hair,

36

There was three pretty maidens awaiting for me,
Saying, 'I will be married on a Tuesday morning.'

On a Tuesday morning the bells they shall ring,
And three pretty maidens so sweetly shall sing;
So neat and so gay in my golden ring,
Saying, 'I will be married on a Tuesday morning.'

This was collected by Cecil Sharp, in 1903. A freer version,
entitled 'I shall be married on Monday morning', was printed
about 1850 on a broadsheet by Williamson of Newcastle. In
1708 it was printed in Walsh's *Twenty-Four New Country
Dances*, under the title 'I mun be marry'd a Tuesday.'

The same thing's happened here as in 'A Ring, A Ring O'
Roses'.* The whole song has been collected after the one-verse
rhyme. Yet it is the more original. It just surfaced later.

The trouble is, although it's the more original, it still isn't
the real original. That must have existed in 1708, 200 years
earlier still, because the tune's title was recorded then. In the
200 years, the Victorians happened. It was their version Cecil
Sharp collected.

They had made the song meaningless. They made the man
meet three pretty girls when he goes to the inn, not just one.
He can't do much with three of them.

Yet this girl had said she was four years single against her
will. That's plain enough. And she'd taunted him – 'You
speak like a man without any skill.' Is that the kind of girl
who would ask two girlfriends along?

She had also told him where she lived. 'The Bonny Blue
Bell' is meaningful, like 'The Black Bull' I mentioned in 'Baa,
Baa, Black Sheep'.* It's the word 'blue' that's supposed to be
a signal, like 'blue joke'. The girl lives in a happy
hunting-ground.

There are two more daft meaninglessnesses put in. One,
that the man went to the pub to powder his locks and curl his
hair. The other, that the three maidens shall be 'So neat and so
gay in my golden ring' at the wedding. What it means I don't

* Both these are in my book *Who Really Killed Cock Robin?*

know, and I don't think whoever wrote it did either. Muddle is also censorship.

The Victorians wanted to hide the real story. They wanted to be respectable – get the girl married before she got slept with. They even got her married on a Sunday – the one day which is impossible for anyone to get married on.

The simple truth is, she is a girl who said 'Yes'. And the Victorians were frightened of her example. She might meet a fate worse than death.

So they muddled up the two days, the day of the night visit, and the day of the wedding. For the wedding day, we're offered a choice of three – Sunday, Monday or Tuesday. All they want is the wedding to be before, or on the same day as, the night visit.

But the girl is an innocent optimist. She hopes the man will marry her after the visit. And her innocence is so foolish, according to Victorian thinking, that the song of it must be made sweet, golden and incomprehensible.

Maybe Tuesday
(Restored)

As I was a-walking one Sunday in the spring,
To hear blackbirds whistle and the skylarks to sing,
I heard a fair maiden, fresh in the dawning,
Singing, 'I will be married on a Monday morning.'

Chorus:
Oh, I will be married on a Monday morning.

I stepped up to her and then softly I did say,
'Pray tell me your age and the place where you stay.'
'At the Bonny Blue Bell sixteen years forlorning,
Singing, "I will be married on a Monday morning." '

Chorus:
Oh, I will be married on a Monday morning.

'Sixteen, pretty maiden, you're too young yet to marry,
I will leave you another four years more to tarry.
You need not till then be so lovelorning,
Singing, "I will be married on a Monday morning." '

Chorus:
Oh, I will be married on a Monday morning.

She said 'You are talking without your manly skill,
These four years I'm single all against my own will.
Each night I'm alone in my bed imploring,
Singing, "I will be married on a Monday morning." '

Chorus:
Oh, I will be married on a Monday morning.

That Sunday, at night-time, I went visiting her there,
She had undone her smock, and she had loosened her hair,
She was waiting for me, herself all adorning,
Singing, 'I will be married on a Monday morning.'

Chorus:
Oh, I will be married on a Monday morning.

Morning, on the Monday, the bell it struck the ten,
This damsel so sweetly she did sing once again,
So gladly, so gaily, without any scorning,
Singing, 'I will be married on a Tuesday morning.'

Chorus:
Oh, I will be married on a Tuesday morning.

The Gardener and I
No. 322, ODNR

There was a man of double deed
Sowed his garden full of seed.
When the seed began to grow,
'Twas like a garden full of snow;
When the snow began to melt,
'Twas like a ship without a belt;
When the ship began to sail,
'Twas like a bird without a tail;
When the bird began to fly,
'Twas like an eagle in the sky;
When the sky began to roar,
'Twas like a lion at the door;
When the door began to crack,
'Twas like a stick across my back;
When my back began to smart,
'Twas like a penknife in my heart;
When my heart began to bleed,
'Twas death and death and death indeed.

> (1784 – first sixteen lines. The dating of final couplet is uncertain.)

If we can understand the 'double deed', we can restore all the imagery.

The narrative proceeds from the 'seed [which] began to grow', through various transformations, to 'my back began to smart' and 'my heart began to bleed'. These are very physical sensations. So strongly are they felt that, for the first time, the narrator loses his control and says 'my' instead of keeping up his impersonality.

From 'seed' to 'my back began to smart' already suggests the meaning. That suggestion is continued by finding the phallic 'bird without a tail' as one of the transformations. When that bird begins to fly, it is like an eagle indeed! Or a lion. And these two lead on to the 'door [which] began to crack'. That, I think, is an image of a woman.

I think, then, that this is a poem about orgasm. The images I have to restore are the 'garden full of snow' and the 'ship without a belt'. I must also correct the babyishness of 'penknife'.

The Gardener and I

(Restored)

Music © Gloria Newton

There was a man of double deed
Who sowed his garden full of seed,
And when the seed began to grow,
'Twas like a pillar made of snow,
'Twas like a pillar made of snow.

When the snow began to slip,
'Twas like a shining, silver ship,
And when the ship began to sail,
'Twas like a bird without a tail,
'Twas like a bird without a tail.

When the bird began to fly,
'Twas like an eagle in the sky,
And when the sky began to roar,
'Twas like a lion at the door,
'Twas like a lion at the door.

When the door began to crack,
'Twas like a stick across my back,
And when my back began to smart,
'Twas like a dagger in my heart,
'Twas like a dagger in my heart.

When my heart began to thump,
'Twas life and death in every jump,
And when my heart began to bleed,
'Twas life and death and life indeed,
'Twas life and death and life indeed.

The Little Coat
No. 187, ODNR

When I was a little girl,
About seven years old,
I hadn't got a petticoat,
To keep me from the cold.

So I went into Darlington,
That pretty little town,
And there I bought a petticoat,
A cloak, and a gown.

I went into the woods
And built me a kirk,
And all the birds of the air,
They helped me to work.

The hawk, with his long claws,
Pulled down the stone,
The dove, with her rough bill,
Brought me them home.

The parrot was the clergyman,
The peacock was the clerk,
The bullfinch played the organ,
And we made merry work.

(1853)

OTHER VERSIONS:
The only other version is from Scotland, and has a tune,
'Lennox Love to Blantyre'.

When I was a wee thing,
'Bout six or seven year auld,
I had no worth a petticoat
To keep me frae the cauld.

Then I went to Edinburgh,
To bonnie burrows town,
And there I *coft* a petticoat   [bought]
A kirtle, and a gown.

As I cam hame again
I thought I wad *big* a kirk,   [build]
And a' the fowls o' the air
Wad help me to work.

The heron, wi' her lang *neb*   [beak]
She *moupit* me the stanes;   [mumble]
The *doo*, wi' her rough legs,   [dove]
She led me them hame.

The *gled* he was a wily thief,   [kite]
I Ie *rackled* up the wa';   [heaped]
The *pyat* was a curst thief   [magpie]
She *dang* down a'.   [knocked]

The hare came *hirpling* owre the knowe   [limping]
To ring the morning bell;
The *hurcheon* she came after,   [hedgehog]
And said she wad do't hersel.

The herring was the high priest,
The salmon was the clerk,
The howlet read the order –
They held a bonnie *wark*.   [work]

Here's another little girl. This time, her age is given. No one is
to doubt that she's too young. But ... her actions are not
those of a seven-year-old. She gets the petticoat, goes into the
woods, builds a kirk (whatever that means) and – last line –
'We made merry work'. We ... in the woods ... petticoat.

The age given is a deliberate lie, to put the reader off. It's an
alteration of the original 'about seventeen years old'. If we'd
read that, we would, of course, have been alerted – ready to
see the meaning of building a kirk and buying a petticoat. For
a petticoat does not keep anyone from the cold. As soon as

she's got this one, off she goes into the woods and makes merry work. Church-building? Funny petticoat, funny church, warm work.

Funny birds, too. There was, once, a whole 'language' of birds. There still is a 'language' of flowers – roses for passion, violets for shyness. And we still know the meaning of the stork. But the meaning of the other birds has been forgotten. We have to work it out. 'The bullfinch played the organ.' Once we're looking for double meaning, there are enough clues left to find it. (There has to be double meaning, because real birds don't build churches.)

We have to understand what these birds are playing at. The hawk has long claws. He pulls down the stone(s). 'Long' is the clue, for we still know 'stones'. Length pulls down the rolling stones, and then the dove (of love) brings them home to the girl. With a rough bill. It's a rough and ready love-making. Length and stones fit in.

Love-making, then, is what the song is all about, told through birds (and animals, too, in the Scotch version). We are meant to see through the petticoat to the hare beneath.

After all, no girl goes into woods with new clothes to do building work. But many girls do go into woods, with a new sexual outfit, to make a predestined meeting with a cock.

There's something to make the folk sing! And they'd understand all the descriptions. They'd know that Darlington was chosen because it's the town of darlings. The same as Edinburgh is the town of bonny burrows. And this petticoat, this little coat? It's the sign of her being seventeen, her sexual hair. That's why the peacock displays his tail. Does the parrot say 'Pretty Polly'?

Some Victorian added the cloak and gown as further cover. But, do girls of seven (or six, which is given in 'Lennox Love to Blantyre') go shopping on their own? So often, the coverings don't stand cross-examination.

The rest of the song is much as it was. But we are not used to fables about birds and beasts any more. So we thought the song was childish nonsense.

The Little Coat

(Restored)

Music © 1984 Chris Howse

Oh when I was a little girl
'Bout sixteen years old,
I hadn't got a little coat
To keep me from the cold.

So off I went to Darlington,
That lively, loving town,
And there I got a little coat
A furry coat of brown.

Then I went warmly to the woods
To build my lad a kirk,
And all the birdies of the air
They helped us with the work.

The hawk with his long, curling claws
He pulled up the round stones,
The dove with her rough nest of love
She brought them firmly home.

The cock he was a canny chief
He raised the tower-wall.
The magpie was a cunning thief –
Stole a ruby to cap all.

The robin was our red, high priest,
The peacock was the clerk,
The bullfinch played the organ
As we made our merry work.

Little Johnny Jig Jag
No. 277, ODNR

Little John Jiggy Jag,
He rode a penny nag,
And went to Wigan to woo;
When he came to a beck,
He fell and broke his neck,
Johnny, how dost thou now?

I made him a hat,
Of my coat lap,
And stockings of pearly blue;
A hat and a feather,
To keep out cold weather,
So, Johnny, how dost thou now?

(1844)

It is his name that does it. John Jiggy Jag jogs. He 'trots behind and ambles before'. He must be the same Johnny who went to Banbury Cross (see p. 94).

This time, he bought a penny nag for himself. But a penny nag is still a horse and will still raise a gallop.

When he came to a beck
He fell and broke his neck.

He must have been galloping fast. As every man is, when he reaches that beck.

Are we wrong? Are we imagining it? We are not imagining 'went to woo'. That's the one plain statement in this story. All the others are double-meaning. So hang on to that 'to woo' and interpret all the others. Even Wigan. It's the place with a wig on.

Now come the 'I' telling the rest of the story. Who is it? Someone who sets him up again. Someone makes him a hat, and stockings of 'pearly blue'. Let's say 'pearly white' because pearly can't go with blue. Johnny has a top hat, and long stockings of pearly white, and a feather (to tickle with), all from this 'I'. From this fine lady with rings on her fingers! She made the hat rise from her lap.

This rhyme isn't another version of 'Ride A Cock Horse.' It's the same story, told in another way. By the woman.

It's a recurrent theme in folk-art, because it re-occurs in life.

Little Johnny Jig Jag
(Restored)

Little Johnny Jig Jag
Rode upon his little nag,
And came up to Wigan to woo.
When he got to a beck,
He jumped and broke his neck.
So, Johnny, what can you do?

I made him a red cap
As he lay in my lap,
And a white stocking he quickly grew.
He had fur and feather
To keep out cold weather.
So Johnny is up again, new.

White Bird Featherless
No. 47, ODNR

White bird featherless
Flew from Paradise,
Pitched on the castle wall;
Along came Lord Landless,
Took it up handless,
And rode away horseless to the King's white hall.

(1855)

OTHER VERSIONS:
This is both very old – a Latin version is from the tenth century – and widespread. There are even earlier Swedish and German folk-versions – proving that the rhyme was known by the Germanic peoples before the Angles and Saxons left home.

Two German versions are much the same. I quote the older one, collected in 1653:

Es flog ein vogel federlosz,
Auff einen Baumb blattlosz,
Da kam die Fraw mundtlosz,
Und frasz den vogel federlosz.

My translation is 'There flew a bird featherless/On a tree leafless/Then came the wife mouthless/And ate the bird featherless.'

It's been out in the cold long enough! The Victorians made it into 'a riddle of the snow and the sun' (ODNR). But the German versions prove that wrong. They say 'wife' where nanny says 'Lord'. They say she ate the bird. They prove that originally this was a rhyme of sexual 'eating' and that the 'white bird featherless' is a male symbol.

The nursery rhyme has deliberately changed the sex of the taker, to censor the rhyme.

White Bird Featherless

(Restored)

White bird featherless
Flew down from Paradise
And perched on the castle wall.
Out came Maid Toothless,
Took him up handless,
And he flew in, wingless,
To the great inner hall.

Rub-A-Dub-Dub!
Three Maids in a Tub!
No. 460, ODNR

Rub-a-dub-dub,
Three men in a tub,
And how do you think they got there?
The butcher, the baker,
The candlestick maker,
They all jumped out of a rotten potato,
'Twas enough to make a man stare.

(1825)

OTHER VERSIONS:

Hey! rub-a-dub, ho! rub-a-dub, three maids in a tub,
And who do you think were there?
The butcher, the baker, the candlestick-maker,
And all of them gone to the fair.

(1798)

The Brewer, the Baker, the Candle-stick-maker

(1830)

Rub-a-dub-dub.
Three men in a tub,
The brewer, the baker, the candlestick-maker,
They all sprung out of a rotten potato.
An apple for the king, a pear for the queen,
And a good toss over the bowling-green.
The bowling-green it was so high,
It nearly tossed me over the sky,
Sky – sky – Let the cat die.

(1892)

This is a good example of censorship. The nursery rhyme of
1798 was made infantile in 1825. 'Three men' were substituted
for 'three maids' in the tub; and they 'jumped out of a rotten

potato' instead of going to the fair.

Three tradesmen have gone to the fair, and seen three maids in a tub ... 'Hey! rub-a-dub! Ho! rub-a-dub!' That surely sounds like the beginning of an exciting verse! But censorship washed out what followed. Only the last source has any kind of ending – and I do restore its version of the conclusion, far though it is from being the continuation of the maids-in-the-bath story.

However, even though no version has any further indication of the bath's progress, I think it can all be deduced from that single opening stanza. 'My end is my beginning.' For the only reason for particularizing the trade each was master of, was so that he could follow it. Each, in turn, would carry on his craft with the maids in the tub.

A choice of tradesman must be made. Two versions have 'butcher', two have 'brewer'. The difference is that the brewer is creative, while the butcher suggests brides-in-the-bath butchery. I think he was wrongly included, even in the earliest version, because the usual linking of butcher and baker was too strong. I'd think that was forgetfulness rather than censorship.

So, with the brewer as my chosen leader of the trio, I composed four verses to follow the text of only one. If finding only one verse where I think there should have been five is like finding a hat on top of a bog, I have dug up the bog burial. Perfectly preserved? Perfectly made? Let us say – I have done as a museum curator does, when a missing portion of some archaeological discovery is continued on the background of the exhibit.

Rub-A-Dub-Dub!
Three Maids in a Tub!

(Restored – 1st version)

Rub-a-dub-dub! Three maids in a tub!
And who do you think came there?
The Brewer, the Baker, the Candlestick-maker,
The three of them came to the fair.

Rub-a-dub-dub! three maids in a tub!
And what did the Brewer do there?
He brewed up a mashing all frothing and splashing
Inside a round barrel all bare.

Rub-a-dub-dub! two maids in a tub!
And what did the Baker do there?
He put in his peel as far as 'twould feel,
Inside a hot oven all bare.

Rub-a-dub-dub! one maid in a tub!
And what did the Candlestick-maker?
He waxed up a candle as long as a handle
And plunged in a holder all bare.

Rub a dub dub! three tups in a tub!
And who do you think left there?
The Brewer, the Baker, the Candlestick-maker,
And none of them nothing to wear!

Rub-A-Dub-Dub! Three Maids in a Tub!

(Restored – 2nd version)

Rub-a-dub-dub!
Three maids in a tub!
The Brewer, the Baker, the Candlestick-maker,
They were all eyes, like a rotten potato.

A pear for the King,
An apple for the Queen,
And a good lay on the bowling-green.
The bowling green it was so high,
It nearly tossed me over the sky.
Sky – sky – let the cat die.

Pippin Hill
No. 417, ODNR

As I was going up Pippen Hill,
Pippen Hill was dirty.
There I met a pretty miss
And she dropt me a curtsey.

Little miss, pretty miss,
Blessings light upon you!
If I had half a crown a day,
I'd spend it all upon you

(1810)

OTHER VERSIONS:
Later versions give either the second verse only or the first
verse only.

It can be restored, once it's read critically. For too long, we've
not questioned anything called a nursery rhyme. This one's
almost religious ... isn't it?

Why does the narrator say he'd spend half a crown a day on
her? Spend? There's been no mention of spending, or of
money, before that.

Why is he so overwhelmed with her politeness that he
blesses her? She only dropped him a curtsey. Yet,
immediately, blessings and riches! Why?

The first verse is trying to tell us why. Because it's all
happening on Pippin Hill, not Pippen Hill. That's the apple-
tree hill, the symbolic, sexual hill – for apple-trees have already
carried that meaning in 'Upon Paul's Steeple'* and will carry it
again in 'Old Roger'.* That's why this sexual hill is 'dirty'. For
over 150 years, 'dirty' must have been used to mean 'sexual' –
what a sign of repression, in itself! For, if it merely meant
'muddy', that description would have to be followed up in the
story. But it isn't. Is sexually dirty followed up? Yes – 'If I had
half a crown a day, I'd spend it all upon you.'

56

On notorious Pippin Hill, a girl drops someone a curtsey. A man? Yes, because it's almost certainly a man who says 'Pretty miss'. What kind of a girl would he say that to? It's a familiar-derogatory form of address. If, in Hyde Park, a pretty girl says 'Hullo!' to a man and he replies 'Hullo, pretty one!', that isn't all politeness.

We can guess the man's age, too, by the 'If I had half a crown a day', because that shows he has not got half a crown a day. He is not rich. So he is not old. (The logic may be more poetic than prosaic.)

Then this young man says that, if he had it, he'd spend all his money on her. What has happened? She must have said something to him which overwhelmed him with joy, something about money, which would make the half-crown buy a lot – and all her speech has been left out of the text. It's because there is no bonding middle verse that the rhyme is disintegrating. The bad join I seek has been found.

Only 'little' is holding back acceptance of the meaning. It does not mean 'young'. The girl is first called 'pretty'. Only in the second verse does that familiar 'little' obstruct understanding. But 'Little Dicky Delver/Had a wife of silver'.* 'Little Bo-peep'* has two daughters. This miss is more pretty than juvenile.

Pippin Hill

(Restored)

As I was going up Pippin Hill,
Pippin Hill was dirty,
There I met a pretty miss
And she dropt me a curtsey.

'Pretty miss, lovesome miss,
May I go with you freely?'
'Young man, never ask me this,
But you may do for a ha'penny!'

---

* The rhymes are given in *Who Really Killed Cock Robin?*

'Pretty miss, winsome miss,
Fortune fall upon you!
If I had half a crown a day,
I'd spend it all upon you!'

The Foolish Owl
No. 393, ODNR

There was an owl lived in an oak,
Wisky, wasky, weedle;
And every word he ever spoke
Was, Fiddle, faddle, feedle.

A gunner chanced to come that way,
Wisky, wasky, weedle;
Says he, I'll shoot you, silly bird,
Fiddle, faddle, feedle.

(1853)

OTHER VERSIONS:
There is a longer version in an earlier (*c.*1805) nursery-rhyme
book:

In an oak there lived an owl,
Frisky, whisky, wheedle!
She thought herself a clever fowl;
Fiddle, faddle, feedle.

*[The next three verses keep the same structure, so I quote lines
1 and 3, only, of them.]*

Her face alone her wisdom shew,
For all she said was, Whit to whoo!

Her silly note a gunner heard,
Says he, I'll shoot you, stupid bird!

Now if he had not heard her hoot,
He had not found her out to shoot.

The tune can be found in *Original Ditties For The Nursery*
(J. Harrise, 1805) or in *Mother Goose's Melodies* (Houghton,
Osgood & Co, 1879).

The sex of the owl? In the earlier version, 'she' in the nursery, becomes 'he'. This is very common metamorphosis – a nursery disguise. The owl must be 'she', because the gunner is 'he'. Gunners don't literally shoot owls. Not even in 1805. Ever eaten stuffed owl? So this masculine gunner is 'shooting' a she-owl, metaphorically.

Confirmation of that metaphor is in what she said, 'Whit to whoo! ... A silly note' – because it sounds like 'To wit, to woo!'. And that's why Shakespeare calls it a 'merry note'. Girls shouldn't reveal their willingness or some gunner may shoot them.

Just in passing, this 'owl in an oak' image must be the same as the 'partridge in the pear tree'. Therefore – for those who collect symbols (i.e. me) – the oak is a male symbol. And when I stood by an oak tree full of acorns, I saw why. But when was the oak a sacred, male tree? In Druid times (just in passing).

The Foolish Owl

(Restored)

There was an owl lived in an oak,
Wibble-y, wobble-y, wibble;
And all the words she ever spoke
Were, Fiddle, faddle, fiddle!

And this was all the sense she knew,
Wibble-y, wobble-y, wibble;
For all she had was 'Wit to woo!'
Fiddle, faddle, fiddle!

Her nightly cry a gunner heard,
Wibble-y, wobble-y, wibble;
He cocked his gun at the round-eyed bird,
Fiddle, faddle, fiddle!

Now if he had not heard her hoot,
Wibble-y, wobble-y, wibble;
He had not found her haunt to shoot,
Fiddle, faddle, fiddle!

The Little Song
No. 326, ODNR

There was a little man,
And he wooed a little maid,
And he said, Little maid, will you wed, wed, wed?
I have little more to say
Than will you, yea or nay?
For the least said is sooner mended, ded, ded.

Then this little maid she said,
Little sir, you've little said,
To induce a little maid for to wed, wed, wed;
You must say a little more,
And produce a little ore
Ere I to the church will be led, led, led.

Then the little man replied,
If you'll be my little bride,
I will raise my love notes a little higher, higher, higher;
Though I little love to prate
Yet you'll find my heart is great,
With the little God of Love all on fire, fire, fire.

Then the little maid replied,
If I should be your bride,
Pray, what must we have for to eat, eat, eat?
Will the flames that you're so rich in
Make a fire in the kitchen,
And the little God of Love turn the spit, spit, spit?

Then the little man he sighed,
And some say a little cried,
And his little heart was big with sorrow, sorrow, sorrow;
I'll be your little slave,
And if the little that I have,
Be too little, little dear, I will borrow, borrow, borrow.

Then the little man so gent,
Made the little maid relent,
And set her little soul a-thinking, king, king;
Though his little was but small,
Yet she had his little all,
And could have of a cat but her skin, skin, skin.

(1765?)

OTHER VERSIONS:
'A Song', 1764, was the first version. The little maiden sings,
in the second verse, 'E'er I make a little print in your bed'.
That is her answer to the first verse, 'Will you say Yes?'

The fourth verse began, 'Then the little maid, she said,
Your fire may warm the bed.' She asks a question and still
does not give permission.

Oh, such a little man! Like a fairy tale. And he wooed a little
maid. It would be a romantic song, wouldn't it? Yes, until it
comes to verse 5.

In that verse, he says he will borrow some more, from
someone else. But can he borrow something from another
person, something physical?

And if the little that I have
Be too little, little dear, I will borrow.

Borrow? Perhaps what was originally said to the 'little girl'
was that she must be able to borrow something, physically,
from someone else. 'You may borrow', instead of 'I will
borrow.' Impossible to think of 'I will borrow.' So that is the
end of comicality.

In the last verse, the poet has 'so gent', to rhyme with
'relent'. That's a funny rhyme. It should want to rhyme with
'urgent'. We see what the rhyme is for, to make her have a
'little soul a-thinking, king, king'. But the 'king' doesn't
rhyme with 'skin'.

There is evidence that the real rhyme has been denied. In
the last line she could have 'of a cat but her skin, skin, skin'.
She could not have it. The girl may have from a female cat her
emblem, which is female, to *possess* it.

What is to happen if it does make sense? If he is trying to persuade a biggish maid?

Could he say (verse 2) 'a little ore' about something masterful? Or will it still be, despite the 'ore', too tiny? It does say in the first version 'Ere I to the church will be led, led, led'; but I respect the version of 1764, 'Ere I make a little print in your bed, bed, bed'. She does say 'Ere'. Then she may get a 'bigger roar', or she may not get one at all. She says you 'make a fire in the kitchen', in the 1764 version; but her 'little print in your bed, bed, bed' will always be uncertain, as she has said, 'Pray, what must we have for to eat, eat, eat?' There, the hidden question was a sexual one. The answer does not rhyme; 'eat' does not rhyme with 'spit'. It needs 'meat'.

If the little man is shown too little, he is shown too little in a double sense – which will not suit a maid. In that sense, it will be sung as the song should be sung. The girl has thought it over, and she has given it a 'little thinking all within, in, in'; and she has decided she will borrow from other men 'a lot of fur, and furkin, kin, kin'. That is the missing rhyme.

She has made her mind up. At most, the little ties up with the little something, too.

The Little Song
(Restored)

There was a little man,
And he loved a little maid,
And he said, 'Little maiden, will you wed, wed, wed?
I have little for a wife,
For I have but little life,
And little life the sooner will be sped, sped, sped.'

Then replied this little maid,
'Little sir, you've little said,
To make a little maiden for to wed, wed, wed.
You must press a little more,
And produce a little roar,
Ere I make a little print in your bed, bed, bed.'

The the little man replied,
'If you will be my little bride,
I will raise my little roar higher, higher, higher;
Though I little love to prate,
Yet you'll find my heat is great,
When the little god of love is all on fire, fire, fire.'

Then the little maiden said,
'Though your heat may warm the bed,
May we find a little something for to eat, eat, eat?
Will the flames that you're so rich in
Light the fire in my kitchen,
And the little god of love give us meat, meat, meat?'

Then the little man he sighed,
And some say a little cried,
And his little heart was big with sorrow, sorrow, sorrow;
'I will be your little slave,
And if the little that I have
Is too little, you may borrow, borrow, borrow!'

Then the little man urgent,
Made the little maid relent,
And a little set her thinking all within, in, in.
Though his roar was but a little small
Yet she'd have it, skin and all,
And could borrow a lot more of fur, and furkin, kin, kin!

Billy Boy
No. 45, ODNR

Where have you been all the day,
My boy Billy?
Where have you been all the day,
My boy Billy?
I have been all the day
Courting of a lady gay;
Although she is a young thing
And just come from her mammy.

Is she fit to be thy love,
My boy Billy?
Is she fit to be thy love,
My boy Billy?
She's as fit to be my love
As my hand is for my glove,
Although she is a young thing
And just come from her mammy.

Is she fit to be thy wife,
My boy Billy?
Is she fit to be thy wife,
My boy Billy?
She's as fit to be my wife,
As my blade is for my knife;
Although she is a young thing
And just come from her mammy.

How old may she be,
My boy Billy?
How old may she be,
My boy Billy?
Twice six, twice seven,
Twice twenty and eleven,

Although she is a young thing
And just come from her mammy.

'For me Nancie tickled me fancy, O' me charmin' Billy Boy.'
The folk-club chorus is right. That's the tone. That's the
meaning. The Victorians tried to mislead readers into
thinking Nancy was an innocent young girl and that Billy was
just a boy.

But the song still speaks clear at its beginning:

'I have been all the day
Courting of a lady gay.'

So Billy is more boisterous, and the lady more gay, than they
wanted us to believe.

The Victorians did their work at the end of the song. There,
they left that impression. There, they disguised the girl's age,
so she became unreal and ladylike. None of their daughters
was to be as fit as 'my blade is for my knife' for some Billy
Boy.

'How old may she be?' – and no simple answer is given to
that simple question.

'Twice six, twice seven
Twice twenty and eleven.'

If that's good enough for a folk-song, no wonder folk-songs
are no good. Twelve? Fourteen? Fifty-one? The worst
alteration must be the fifty-one. Fourteen is just possible, but
what about twelve? Twelve must surely be too young, even
for Shakespeare. So, the answer must be *not* twelve, nor
fourteen, but some other age.

The Victorians were influenced by the way that other age
was worded. They kept the 'twice' something, and they kept
the idea of adding a number on to it. The little word 'and' is a
clue. The original they altered must have been 'Not twice six,
nor twice seven/But twice ... and ...'.

Because she is 'a young thing/And just come from her
mammy', her age must be under twenty. So, 'twice eight and
then a one'. Seventeen, sweet seventeen! Now Billy isn't

schoolboyish. He's been away, the whole of a love-long day, courting a Juliet of seventeen. The folk remembered.

And we – we readers – we can restore the details that made their courting strong. It was strong enough to appeal to sailors. The song was a sea-shanty. It's only recently that it's come down to the Boy Scouts. Them, and their little knives.

So, not 'lady gay'. Not 'hand is for my glove'. Not 'blade is for my knife'. The young girl fits. Right on. Right in.

Billy Boy
(Restored)

'Where have you been all the day,
Billy Boy, Billy Boy?
Where have you been all the day,
My Billy Boy?'
'I've been away all day
Courting of me Nancie May,
For me Nancie tickled me fancy
O' me charmin' Billy Boy.'

'Is she fit to be thy love,
Billy Boy, Billy Boy?
Is she fit to be thy love,
My Billy Boy?'
'She's as fit to be my love
As my hand fits in my glove,
For me Nancie tickled me fancy
O' me charmin' Billy Boy.'

'Is she fit to be thy wife,
Billy Boy, Billy Boy?
Is she fit to be thy wife,
My Billy Boy?'
'She's as fit to be my wife
As my sheath fits on my knife,
For me Nancie tickled me fancy
O' me charmin' Billy Boy.'

'Is she fit to sweep thy house,
Billy Boy, Billy Boy?
Is she fit to sweep thy house,
My Billy Boy?'
'She's as fit to sweep my house
As her handle fits my brush,
For me Nancie tickled me fancy
O' me charmin' Billy Boy.'

'Is she fit to make thy cake,
Billy Boy, Billy Boy?
Is she fit to make thy cake,
My Billy Boy?'
'She's as fit to make my cake
As her oven's fit to bake,
For me Nancie tickled me fancy
O' me charmin' Billy Boy.'

'Many years has she been born,
Billy Boy, Billy Boy?
Many years has she been born,
My Billy Boy?'
'Not twice six nor twice seven,
But twice eight and then a one,
For me Nancie took her chancy
O' me charmin' Billy Boy!'

Hill-Billy Boy

(Current American version of 'Billy Boy')
Folk Songs collected in the Appalachian Mountains,
Cecil Sharp

Where have you been, Billy Boy, Billy Boy,
O where have you been, charming Billy?
I have been to seek a wife
For the pleasures of my life;

She's a young girl and cannot leave her mammy.

[The other verses follow this pattern, so I give their new lines only.]

Did she ask you to come in …?
She asked me to come in;
She had a dimple in her chin.

Did she set you in a chair …?
She set me in a chair;
She had wrinkles in her ear.

Did she ask you for to eat …?
She asked me for to eat,
She had plenty bread and meat.

Can she card and can she spin …?
She can card and she can spin,
And can do most anything.

Can she sew and can she fell …?
She can sew and she can fell,
She can use her needle well.

Can she make a cherry pie …?
She can make a cherry pie,
Quick as cat can wink his eye.

How old may be she be …?
She's twice six, twice seven,
Twenty-eight and eleven.

(1917)

The Americans carried on tickling their fancy. Their fancies became different. But Billy is still 'seeking a wife/For the pleasures of my life'.

Fancies and pleasures met the same kind of censorship. The New England Puritans muddled the girl's age in almost the same words as the Victorians did. They were the same kind of people.

Censorship began at the beginning. 'Did she ask you to come in? She did ask me to come in/She had a dimple in her chin.' If the answer was made stupid, they hoped the question would be, too.

But 'Did she ask you to come in?' is not a stupid question. It's direct – as direct as Mae West's 'Come up and see me sometime.' When her man calls, will she ask him to come in?

What should the 'dimple' be? It should be much the same as the 'wrinkle'in the next verse.

'Did she set you in a chair?
She did set me in a chair
She had wrinkles in her ear.'

That's such a bad rhyme it suggests the real answer. 'She had wrinkles in her hair.' Oh! Different hair. Different chair.

The dimple and the wrinkle are both inlets. 'She did ask me to come in,/Through an inlet ... [like a wrinkle] ... And then set me in a chair which had wrinkles in its hair.'

'Plenty bread and plenty meat' – a bountiful girl. 'She can do most anything' – especially one thing. '*Meine Frau kann alles,*' sing the Germans – 'My wife can do everything.' On Friday, she baths. On Saturday, she makes love.

'She can sew and she can fell.' Fell. It may be one of the pleasures of Billy's life that his wife can 'stitch down with an overturned edge' (*Chambers Dictionary*), but I think he'd rather she was overturned and that he did the sowing.

Of course she can use her needle well. It has an open eye.

The 'cherry-pie' has a cherry in. 'I gave my love a cherry/Without any stone' is a current American folk-song – and an English one, too. The cherry must have a bone.

The song has to have its double meanings restored. Without them, all Billy is going to do is sit in a chair, with a snack from the deep-freeze, and watch television while his girl knits. She'll be the one who goes away all day, courting some more meaningful Billy Boy.

Hill-Billy Boy

(Restored)

'Where have you been all the day,
Billy Boy, Billy Boy?
Where have you been all the day,
My Billy Boy?'
'I've been to seek a wife
For the pleasures of me life,
Though she is so very young
To be taken from her mummy.'

'Did she ask you to come in,
Billy Boy, Billy Boy?
Did she ask you to come in,
My Billy Boy?'
'Oh she asked me to come in,
Through a door that's deep and dim,
Though she is so very young
To be taken from her mummy.'

'Did she set you in a chair,
Billy Boy, Billy Boy?
Did she set you in a chair,
My Billy Boy?'
'Oh she set me in a chair
That had wrinkles in its hair,
Though she is so very young
To be taken from her mummy.'

'Did she ask you for to eat,
Billy Boy, Billy Boy?
Did she ask you for to eat,
My Billy Boy?'
'Oh, she asked me for to eat,
And she'd plenty milk and meat,
Though she is so very young
To be taken from her mummy.'

'Did she card and did she spin,
Billy Boy, Billy Boy?
Did she card and did she spin,
My Billy Boy?'
'She did card and she did spin,
She did line with silk within,
Though she is so very young
To be taken from her mummy.'

'Did she sew and did she fell,
Billy Boy, Billy Boy?
Did she sew and did she fell,
My Billy Boy?'
'She did sew and she did fell,
She did use her needle well,
Though she is so very young
To be taken from her mummy.'

'Did she make a cherry pie,
Billy Boy, Billy Boy?
Did she make a cherry pie
My Billy Boy?'
'She did make a cherry pie,
And she'll bake it bye and bye,
Though she is so very young
To be taken from her mummy.'

'What's the age of this young girl,
Billy Boy, Billy Boy?
What's the age of this young girl
My Billy Boy?'
'Not twice six nor twice seven
But twice eight and then a one,
Oh, but what she's gone and done
To be taken from her mummy!'

Hunting the Wren
No. 447, ODNR

We will go to the wood, says Robin to Bobbin,
We will go to the wood, says Richard to Robin,
We will go to the wood, says John all alone,
We will go to the wood, says everyone,

What to do there? says Robin to Bobbin,
What to do there? says Richard to Robin,
What to do there? says John all alone,
What to do there? says everyone.

We'll shoot at a wren, says Robin to Bobbin, *etc.*

She's down, she's down, says Robin to Bobbin, *etc.*

Then pounce, then pounce, says Robin to Bobbin, *etc.*

She is dead, she is dead, says Robin to Bobbin, *etc.*

How get her home? says Robin to Bobbin, *etc.*

In a cart with six horses, says Robin to Bobbin, *etc.*

Then hoist, boys, hoist, says Robin to Bobbin, *etc.*

How shall we dress her? says Robin to Bobbin, *etc.*

We'll hire seven cooks, says Robin to Bobbin, *etc.*

How shall we boil her? says Robin to Bobbin, *etc.*

In the brewer's big pan, says Robin to Bobbin,
In the brewer's big pan, says Richard to Robin,
In the brewer's big pan, says John all alone,
In the brewer's big pan, says everyone.

(c. 1744)

OTHER VERSIONS:
Dibyn, Dobyn, Risiart, Robin, John

(Welsh version)

Brothers-in-Three

(Ireland)

Johnie Rednosie ... brither and kin

(Scotland)

John in the Long

(England)

Details of the story from the various countries are:

We'll shoot at a wren
With great guns and cannon.

(England)

What way will ye get her in?
Drive down the door-cheeks.

(Scotland)

[She'll give] eyes to the blind, legs to the lame, and pluck to
the poor.

(Isle of Man)

The Manx would also invite the King and the Queen to the
wren banquet.

The custom of hunting the wren was kept up in France and
Scandinavia, as well as Britain. It stems from pre-Christian
times. The first missionaries objected to it. The Druids held
the bird sacred. The hunt was still taking place in Ireland in
1946.

The men garlanded the body, then bore it in triumph back
to the village, while chanting the words.

It's a woman hunt. That's why the lads and men chase the
bird for miles over the countryside. Then they carry her body
back in triumph to the village. 'We've got one!'

They are mock-serious about it all. They go to shoot this,

the smallest of birds, with great guns and cannon! With themselves, of course, slightly exaggerated. They bring her home in a cart with six horses. A wren!

Wren for woman, Robin for man, is the foundation of all bird-symbolism. The wren was chosen as the woman-bird because she has a jutting-out little tail, and a round nest with a hole in it, lined with moss inside. What more can any primitive man want? Robin was chosen as man's own badge because of his reddish breast. Dark red – blood red – is the true phallic colour; and the robin's the only bird that has something like it on display. (The bull-finch also shows some red. That's why he's the bull-finch.)

'Robin' became the favourite man's name. 'Jenny' became the favourite woman's name. The birds were loved, for they were every married couple – though country people knew perfectly well, then as now, that robins don't mate with wrens. Feelings over-ride facts.

Other birds joined the prime pair. The stork brought babies in his long bill, and the peacock showed and shook his tail (both birds are in 'The Little Coat' earlier on). The lark rose early in the morning. Today, 'birds' have lost much of their individuality; and we say 'birds' to mean women in general. Now, if we want a bird to be male, we have to say 'cock' in front of the bird's name 'Whatcher, me old cock sparrow!'

But we still put robins on Christmas cards, and by so doing we keep the link with the Druids and with this chant. For robin was their king-bird, and the wren was the queen. So, on 25 December, the day of the sun's return, the king-deputy (Robin) led the hunt for his queen – for all women. The hunt was to help the sun rise again, for the sun was a male god and, like any other man, needed his virility confirmed. His return was not just a natural fact. It was a human one. It was linked with unconquerability and potency.

Robin leads the hunt as chief male member. And his two companions are also male members, men and more-than-men. They're called Robin and Bobbin, or Dibbin and Dobbin, because they are a pair. They are the testicles – just as Robin, being phallic, can be called John the Rednose.

Together, Robin and his two partners are the first Trinity,

the lucky Three of fertility. From this trio comes the folk-saying 'All good things come in threes.' The Christians tried to take over the good luck, and so made their Trinity one too many. 'God the Father, yes. God the Son, yes. But God the Holy Ghost, who's he?' So said a mathematical friend. The answer is, he's Dobbin or Dibbin.

The three men-in-one hunt a woman. They pounce on her as she lies. And then they learn 'the vast size of the quarry', as the ODNR puts it. A man may boast he's bigger than a woman – of his great piece of artillery – until he finds out. There must have been married men in the hunt.

Now we can understand why the wren is fit for the king's banquet.

A woman – desire of a woman – will give eyes to the blind, legs to the lame, and pluck to the poor. Blind men, lame men, poor men, will go on the hunt. Every year, a poor old half-blind tom cat used to come limping up our garden path after our female cat. His bird-hunting, though, was not symbolic.

What's the end of the men's wren hunt? It's not her death. The chant goes on after she's been pounced on. It's 'How shall we boil her? In the brewer's big pan.' What that means is, 'How shall we settle her down? In the pudding club's pan.' For the brewer made things swell up, froth and ferment. In Ireland, the brewers even make a 'creature'. When the wren becomes pregnant, that's the rightful end of the hunt.

Hunting the Wren

(Restored)

'Let us go to the wood,' says Robin the Bobbin';
'Let us go to the wood,' says Dibbin 'n Dobbin;
'Let us go to the wood,' says John in the Long;
'Let us go to the wood,' says everyone.

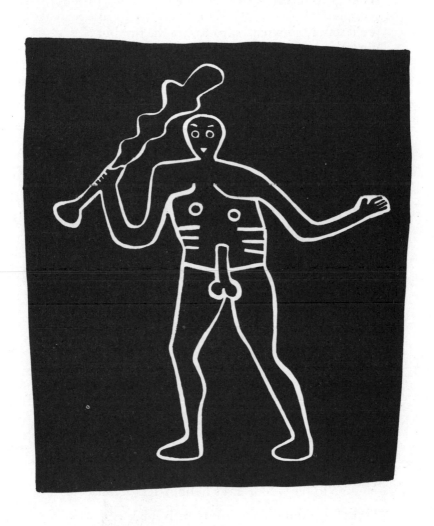

'What to do there?' says Robin the Bobbin';
'What to do there?' says Dibbin 'n Dobbin;
'What to do there?' says John in the Long;
'What to do there?' says everyone.

'We'll shoot at a wren,' says Robin the Bobbin';
'We'll shoot at a wren,' says Dibbin 'n Dobbin;
'We'll shoot at a wren,' says John in the Long;
'We'll shoot at a wren,' says everyone.

'What with? What with?' says Robin the Bobbin'; *etc.*

'With great guns and cannon,' says Robin the Bobbin'; *etc.*

'She's down! She's down!' says Robin the Bobbin'; *etc.*

'Fall on her! Fall on her!' says Robin the Bobbin'; *etc.*

'She's dead! She's dead!' says Robin the Bobbin'; *etc.*

'How draw her home?' says Robin the Bobbin'; *etc.*

'In a cart with six horses,' says Robin the Bobbin'; *etc.*

'How get her in?' says Robin the Bobbin'; *etc.*

'Drive down the door-cheeks!' says Robin the Bobbin'; *etc.*

'How shall we cook her?' says Robin the Bobbin'; *etc.*

'Hire seven cooks and their scullions!' says Robin the
Bobbin'; *etc.*

'Who's the dish fit for?' says Robin the Bobbin'; *etc.*

''Tis fit for a king!' says Robin the Bobbin'; *etc.*

'What's the dish good for?' says Robin the Bobbin'; *etc.*

'She'll give legs to the lame!' says Robin the Bobbin'; *etc.*

'What more's the dish good for?' says Robin the Bobbin';
etc.

'She'll give eyes to the blind!' says Robin the Bobbin'; *etc.*

'And what more's the dish good for?' says Robin the
Bobbin'; *etc.*

'She'll give pluck to the poor!' says Robin the Bobbin'; *etc.*

'Then, how shall we boil her?' says Robin the Bobbin'; *etc.*

'In the pudding club's pan!' says Robin the Bobbin';
'In the pudding club's pan!' says Dibbin 'n Dobbin;
'In the pudding club's pan!' says John in the Long;
'In the pudding club's pan!' says everyone.

Marriage Rhymes

Wedding Wish
No. 189, ODNR

Gray goose and gander,
Waft your wings together,
And carry the good king's daughter
Over the one-strand river.

(1844)

Does she mean it literally that the goose and gander will fly away with her over the river to some happy place? Is she a fairy princess in some story of Mother Goose? Or is she a very human girl, speaking poetically?

If her words can be understood, she'll come alive like the Sleeping Beauty. Her poetry will be meaningful.

Goose and gander are a pair, a pair of good old sex-symbols for man and woman. 'What's sauce for the goose is sauce for the gander' is a proverbial use of them.

'Oh, pair of good old sex-symbols, sweep lightly and smoothly along ['waft' in the *Concise Oxford Dictionary*], and carry me, the good king's daughter, over the one-strand river.'

What river's got only one strand to it? What river's got the open sea beyond? Where will the sex symbols naturally fly to?

They'll fly over the girl's virginity, over her river. And then where? For the rhyme should go on. They'll take her to the land of happy marriage.

The girl has been wishing deeply, praying, in the folk way, before her wedding. 'Waft your wings together, so we'll be flying together, in harmony, my husband and I.'

The rhyme was said when throwing-up and catching a baby (*London Treasury of NR*). When the prayer had been answered, it could be spoken aloud.

She calls herself 'the good king's daughter' because of the exalted state of mind she's in. Don't we still half-think a girl on her wedding-day is a queen? 'The King of Spain's daughter/Came to visit me.' That was some other girl, some other English girl, coming to visit some Prince Charming.

King and Queen of Cantylon
How far is it to Babylon?

Men become kings, too, at supreme moments in their lives.
What we have to do is carry her prayer to its proper end. So she can say it to the baby. Someone cut it short because they didn't want 'one-strand river' understood. Nothing sexual, no matter how beautiful and fitting, was to be passed on. Silence like the grave.

Wedding Wish
(Restored)

Gray goose and gander
Waft your wings together,
And carry the good king's daughter
Over the one-strand river.
Set her on the other side,
A happy wife, a fruitful bride.

Down in the Ditch
No. 310, ODNR

Here goes my lord,
A trot, a trot, a trot, a trot …
Here goes my lady,
A canter, a canter, a canter, a canter …
Here goes my young master,
Jockey-hitch, jockey-hitch, jockey-hitch, jockey-hitch …
Here goes my young miss,
An amble, an amble, an amble, an amble …
The footman lags behind to tipple ale and wine,
And goes a gallop, a gallop, a gallop, to make up his time.

(1849)

OTHER VERSIONS:
Here comes my lady with her little baby,
A nim, a nim, a nim.
Here comes my lord with his trusty sword,
Trot, trot, trot.
Here comes old Jack with a broken pack,
A gallop, a gallop, a gallop.

(1946)

The second version is the better. It's got the descriptions of my lady, with 'her little baby', and of my lord, with 'his trusty sword', that make the picture. But, where have 'my young miss' and 'my young master' gone?

We'll be able to find them, describe them and place them when we know where the rhyme itself is going. It's going to a gallop. It begins with the slowest pace and constantly quickens it. At the gallop comes old Jack with his broken pack. (Never the footman. He'd never gallop, even if he were late. He's from a Victorian household, grumbling about the servants.)

'Broken pack'? It doesn't make sense. A pack is soft and unbreakable – like a wool-pack in those days, an army pack in ours. And even if Jack did break some sort of kitbag, what's the point of that?

Yet, if he broke his back, that would fit his wild gallop, in both senses, for the pace of the riders is their speed in love. We still use 'fast' in the same way.

Lady with baby, lord with sword, quicken to the galloping of Jack, the wild boy, the lad himself. Not 'old' at all. Only 'old Jack' because we all like him.

So 'sword' was a symbol, to go with 'baby'. The lord's sword was trusty (not rusty!).

Where are we to fit my young miss and my young master into this progression? At the beginning. With the beginners. With the slow pace.

And what are they to come 'with'? They are to come with symbols of their sex that rhyme with 'miss' and 'master'.

They'll start the ride of love, the cavalcade to Canterbury. Young Jack leads the final charge. He falls. The child, bouncing on his knee, falls. He laughs. The child laughs.

Down in the Ditch

(Restored)

Here comes my young miss, with a loving kiss,
An amble, an amble, an amble ...
Here comes my young master, with something faster,
Jockey-(h)itch, jockey-itch, jockey-itch ...
Here comes my lady, with her little baby,
A canter, a canter, a canter ...
Here comes my lord, with his trusty sword,
A trot, a trot, a trot ...
Here comes Wild Jack, he'll break his back!
A gallop, a gallop, a gallop ... Down in the ditch!

This is the Way the Ladies Ride
No. 290, ODNR

This is the way the ladies ride,
Nimble, nimble, nimble, nimble;
This is the way the gentlemen ride,
A gallop a trot, a gallop a trot;
This is the way the farmers ride,
Jiggety jog, jiggety jog;
And when they come to a hedge – they jump over!
And when they come to a slippery place – they scramble,
scramble,
Tumble-down Dick!

(1849)

Right into the ditch.

(1950)

'Nimble'? Nonsense. It was originally 'an amble'. That became 'a-namble'. That turned into 'a-nimble' because someone didn't know the word 'amble'. And here, just 'nimble' stays on its own, for the ladies.

Even that isn't the end of the changes. 'Nimble' becomes the 'nim' of the other version in the previous rhyme, 'Down in the Ditch'.

From an amble to a gallop to a jump. From a hedge to a slippery place to a ditch. To tumble-down Dick. It must be a sexual ride. 'They scramble, they scramble' doesn't fit a sexual meaning? Neither does it fit a non-sexual one. Riders don't fall down after a scramble.

'Scramble' is one alteration. 'Farmers' is another. They don't belong here. They've got no wives. They don't ride faster, or break more hedges, than gentlemen. Their 'jiggety-jog' isn't faster than 'gallop a trot'. It should be – because we're going to raise a good gallop and jump that hedge, get through that slippery place, right into that ditch. It all reminds me of 'The Aborigines performed a ritual dance around a trench dug in the ground, and decorated with bushes. They at first held their spears up between their legs, like phalli, and later they stabbed them repeatedly and vigorously into the trench' (Philip Rawson (ed.), *Primitive Erotic Art*). Their bushes are our hedge, our 'bush'. Their vigorous spears are stabbing into our ditch. One touch of nature makes the whole world kin.

We've rejected the farmers, even with hypothetical farmers' wives. They are not kin to the aboriginal riders. Bring in another pair. Who can go faster than the ladies and gentlemen? Who can go faster than the respectable, settled couples? This time, this rhyme, I thought the young misses and young masters must have increased their speed, for they are the only other entries in this race.

This is the Way the Ladies Ride
(Restored)

This is the way the ladies ride,
An amble, an amble, an amble ...
This is the way the gentlemen ride,
Jig-jog, jig-jog, jig-jog ...
This is the way the young girls ride,
A canter, a canter, a canter ...
This is the way the young men ride,
Giddy-up, giddy-up, giddy-up ...
And when they come to a hedge ... they jump up!
And when they come to a slippery place ... they jump up, up!
And when they come to a ditch ... they jump up, up, up, up, up!
Tumble-down Dick!

John Cook's Mare
No. 276, ODNR

John Cook had a little grey mare,
He, haw, hum!
Her back stood up and her bones were bare,
He, haw, hum!

John Cook was riding up Shuter's Bank,
He, haw, hum!
And there his nag did kick and prank,
He, haw, hum!

John Cook was riding up Shuter's Hill,
He, haw, hum!
His mare fell down and she made her will,
He, haw, hum!

The bridle and saddle he laid on the shelf,
He, haw, hum!
If you want any more you may sing it yourself,
He, haw, hum!

(1810?)

OTHER VERSIONS:
This is a song from 1500. It was sung till at least 1897, for then
its first line was recorded in *Songs of Norfolk* as 'Robin
Cook's wife she had a grey mare.'

I do want some more. Then I'll sing it myself. But the more I
want is not at the very end. It's just before the end. That's
where part of the song is missing.
   There's a gap between 'His mare fell down and she made
her will' and 'The bridle and saddle he laid on the shelf.' Did
she die? What was her will? Where did the shelf come from? I
thought we were out in the country. How can laying bridle
and saddle down be the end of the song?

It can't, at the moment. But it can, if there's something in the missing part which makes his action a foregone conclusion.

When there's a gap, consider both ends. 'His mare fell down and she made her will.' A horse can't make a will. So 'she' isn't a horse. She is Mrs Cook. 'John Cook had a little grey wife. Her back stood up and her bones were bare. On Shuter's Bank, there his wife did kick and prank. [This is pranking, not prancing.] On that same Shuter's Hill, his wife fell down and she made her will.'

The two actions go together, the falling down and the making her will. It's because she's fallen down, deliberately, that she shows what her will is. She wants to be made love to.

And John Cook? He lays his bridle and saddle down somewhere, but not on the shelf. That's a joke, a ridiculous joke. Where he can ride her. The missing part of the song made it obvious what he was going to do.

We've got the sense. Let's make it precise. 'Her back stood up and her bones were bare.' There is only one part of a mare that stands up where a woman does. It's part of her back. A mare's bones aren't bare. None of her is, or all of her is. But Mrs Cook must have one part bare for this riding. Precisely.

'Shuter's Bank' must be spelt 'Shooter's Bank'. Shooting with a big arrow or a little gun has been man's practice from Robin the Bobbin' to James Bond. And the chorus line, too, must be correctly spelt – 'Hee, haw, hum!' – to show this is a humorous, hee-haw song.

Humorous, human, happy! That's a folk-song. The folk sang it for hundreds of years, till the flat Norfolk version eventually forgot all about folk-riding. Mrs Cook never owned a mare. She *was* the mare.

John Cook's Mare

(Restored)

John Cook had a little grey mare,
Hee, haw, hum!
Her bum was broad, and her belly was bare,
Hee, haw, hum!

John Cook was riding up Shooter's Bank,
Hee, haw, hum!
And there his mare did frisk and prank,
Hee, haw, hum!

John Cook was riding up Shooter's Hill,
Hee, haw, hum!
His mare lay down and would have her will,
Hee, haw, hum!

John Cook rose and looked at the mare,
Hee, haw, hum!
Her belly was broad, and her bum was bare,
Hee, haw, hum!

John Cook saw she'd the bit in her teeth,
Hee, haw, hum!
And the saddle was down on her underneath,
Hee, haw, hum!

John Cook put up his whip ... on the shelf,
Hee, haw, hum!
If you want any more you must ride her yourself,
Hee, haw, hum!

Pease Porridge
No. 400, ODNR

Pease porridge hot,
Pease porridge cold,
Pease porridge in the pot
Nine days old.

Some like it hot,
Some like it cold,
Some like it in the pot
Nine days old.

(c. 1797)

This rhyme does not make sense. Who likes cold porridge? Who likes it in the pot, nine days old? So it's semantic porridge! I suppose the derivation of 'peas' is that 'pease porridge' can be hot or cold; and the look of semen being from peas.*

'Pot' is still used to mean stomach, so I can understand that women might like such 'porridge' in the womb. But nine days? The only significant length of time with 'nine' in is nine months.

When that length of time has passed, some would like it. Others won't. It's significant how it makes 'nine days' alter. Nine months change it.

Pease Porridge
(Restored)

Pease porridge hot,
Pease porridge cold,
Pease porridge in the pot
Nine months old.

---

* Partridge says: 'Peas in the pot are apt to be amorous. From 1890.'

All like it hot,
None like it cold,
Some like it in the pot
Nine months old.

Cobbler, Cobbler, Mend My Shoe
No. 103, ODNR

Cobbler, cobbler, mend my shoe.
Yes, good master, that I'll do;
Here's my awl and wax and thread …
And now your shoe is quite mended.

(1805)

OTHER VERSIONS:
Cobbler, cobbler, mend my shoe,
Get it done by half past two.

(1945)

Stitch it up and stitch it down,
And then I'll give you half a crown.

(1948)

Half-past two is much too late,
Get it done by half past eight.

(Current)

'It's all cobblers' means it's all balls, because cobblers have big balls of wax.

The cobbler was a famous tradesman, like our milkman. He not only had the balls, he also had the wherewith-awl and the black hairy thread.

So he mended women's shoes. And to have him mend men's – 'Yes, good master' – is the first sign of alteration. Why should he tell a man 'Here's my awl and wax and thread'? Is the man blind or a simpleton? But to tell a woman would not be such simple talk.

This 'mend my shoe' sets the double-meaning going from the beginning. The shoe was well known as a sign of woman's sex. So 'mend my shoe' was a signal, an invitation. Hence the 'stitch it up and stitch it down'. There'd be no need to specify the up and down of the stitching if the signal were not being given.

'And I will give you half a crown.' That was too much for an ordinary shoe-repair. It was the price of a bed and breakfast in 1939-45. It was also the traditional price of a prostitute. The woman offers too much to show her need.

Her need is matched by his speed. She wants it done quickly. He does it straightaway. His repairing it to fit a stiff upper into a stout sole.

Cobbler, Cobbler, Mend My Shoe
(Restored)

'Cobbler, cobbler, mend my shoe,
Get it done by half past two,
Stitch it up and stitch it down,
And I will give you half a crown.'

'Yes, good mistress, that I'll do,
Straight-a-way, for nothing, too.
Here's my awl and wax and thread ...
And now your hole is well mended.'

Ride a Cock Horse
No. 29, ODNR

Ride a cock horse to Banbury Cross,
To buy little Johnny a galloping horse;
It trots behind and it ambles before,
And Johnny shall ride it till he can ride no more.

(1805)

No. 30, ODNR

Ride a cock horse to Banbury Cross,
To see a fine lady upon a white horse;
Rings on her fingers and bells on her toes,
And she shall have music wherever she goes.

(1844?)

A real horse doesn't last a boy's life-time. A real horse doesn't trot behind and amble before. A real horse is not bought at Banbury Cross in particular. So it isn't a real horse.

It's a galloping horse! That makes all the difference, because 'gallop' and 'ride' are still sexual doing-words. This horse has stood for loving bareback ever since the first man rode one. The motion is the same.

That's why horses were cut on chalk hills. They shone out over the people like the cocks on the church steeples. We have forgotten what the white horse stands for. Not whisky but frisky! Yet we still use 'jump' and 'whip' to go with 'ride' and 'gallop'.

Now, that sort of white horse does last a lad's life-time. It does amble before, though 'trot behind' is wrong. Above all, it is bought from Banbury Cross. For Banbury Cross was 'a goodly, big, Cross' (ODNR). It was specially named as being the particular place to get a goodly, big one.

By a boy bouncing up and down on his father's knee. By a little cock bouncing up and down by a big one. It may 'hang down' but not 'behind'.

The Puritans knocked down the great cross. They knocked down the maypoles too. They must have known what both stood for. They must have understood this rhyme.

It was their early Victorian descendants who knocked the rhyme about a bit. But we will remember the Laughing Cavalier as off we go to the cross again, for the second verse.

This time, for a fine lady. A fine, big one. And what is our fine one wearing? 'Rings on her fingers and bells on her toes.' Only. Then a string of beads and a smile! For the purpose of rings and bells is not only to adorn her nakedness but to make music, to ring out like bells under honeymoon beds. She and Johnny gallop together, the bells ringing out from wild woods and wild beds.

The two verses join together into one adult song. Yet they were two separate nursery rhymes.

'Wherever she goes' means nothing other than 'all her life through'. Just as Johnny will ride the white horse till he can ride no more, so she shall have that music for ever.

Ride a Cock Horse

(Restored)

Ride a cock horse to Banbury Cross
To buy little Johnny a galloping horse.
It jogs, and it jigs, and it jumps on before,
And Johnny shall ride it till he rides no more.

Ride a cock horse to Banbury Cross
To buy a fine lady for Johnny's white horse.
Rings on her fingers and bells on her toes,
She shall have music wherever she goes!

Dance To Your Daddy
No. 123, ODNR

Dance to your daddy,
My little babby,
Dance to your daddy, my little lamb;
You shall have a little fishy
In a little dishy,
You shall have a fishy when the boat comes in.

(1846)

OTHER VERSIONS:
Dance to your daddy,
My little babby,
Dance to your daddy, my little lamb;
And ye'll get a coatie
And a pair o' breekies –
Ye'll get a whippie and a supple tam!

(1842)

An' a whirligiggie an a supple Tam.

(1842)

Baby shall have an apple,
Baby shall have a plum,
Baby shall have a rattle,
When Daddy comes home.

(1844)

An' ye'll get a slicie o' a dishie nicey,
An' a sweetie wiggie, an' a mutton ham.

(1928)

Come here my little Jackey,
Now I've smoked my baccy,
Let's have a bit of crackey
Till the boat comes in.

Dance to thy daddy, sing to thy mammy,
Dance to thy daddy, to thy mammy sing;
Thou shalt have a fishy on a little dishy,
Thou shalt have a fishy when the boat comes in.

> (Composed by William Watson, *The Newcastle Song Book*, 1842)

Here is the Holy Family as it really is. The Dad is singing out his sexual happiness over the head of the naked baby to the listening mother. Here is the promise of sexual fulfilment, passed from father to son.

The baby is dancing to his daddy, who is not at sea, or on a fishing-boat. Dad is at home, singing to his son, after he's bathed and dried him.

The song must fit that setting.

'You shall have a fishy
On a little dishy.'

There's the misfit. There's the alteration. The setting says 'in'. The William Watson version, which made the rhyme into the current song, says 'on'. The song-writer changed the rhyme, made it respectable and publishable, by making the baby older and by putting 'on'. The baby is to have a real fish for dinner. That's respectable realism. Will the baby choke?

'When the boat comes in' does not mean 'When your father's fishing-boat lands'. It does mean 'When the good times come – when you're grown up'. 'Fishy', of course, does fit fishing-boat. But most of the other things the baby will get do not. Neither coatie, nor pair o' breekies, nor apple, plum, nor rattle, nor whippie and supple Tam. Supple Tam goes with a 'slicie o' a dishie nicie'.

'On a little dishy' is flat on a plate. But 'in a little dishy' is not flat. For 'dish' means woman, then as now. And the fishy fits that meaning. That can be the only reason why the baby should get a supple Tam. Now we're seeing the imagery, that's why he'll get a red apple, a purple plum and a rattling rattle! He'll get a nice wife like I've got. That's what Dad is singing. His son will have the same things he himself now has.

The song must be restored to its setting. The baby will not understand. But the mother will.

Dance to Your Daddy

(Restored)

Dance to your daddy,
My little laddy,
Dance to your daddy,
To your mammy sing.
You shall have a fishy
In a little dishy,
You shall have a swishy
When your ship comes in.

Dance to your daddy,
My little laddy,
Dance to your daddy,
To your mammy sing.
You shall have a slice-y
Of a pie so nice-y,
You shall have some spice-y
When your ship comes in.

Dance to your daddy,
My little laddy,
Dance to your daddy,
To your mammy sing.
You shall have an apple,
And a little rattle,
You'll have some tittle-tattle
When your ship comes in.

Dance to your daddy,
My little laddy,
Dance to your daddy,
To your mammy sing.
You shall have a jiggy,
And a whirlygiggy,

You shall have a biggy
When your ship comes in.

Dance to your daddy,
My little laddy,
Dance to your daddy,
To your mammy sing.
You shall have a mammy,
And a little rammy,
And a supple Tammy
When your ship comes in!

The Jerkin and the Petticoat
The Puffin Book of Nursery Rhymes

As I went by my little pig-sty,
I saw a child's petticoat hanging to dry,
Hanging to dry, hanging to dry,
I saw a child's petticoat hanging to dry.

I took off my jacket and hung it close by,
To bear that petticoat company,
Company, company,
To bear that petticoat company.

The wind blew high and down they fell,
Jacket and petticoat into the well,
Into the well, into the well,
Jacket and petticoat into the well.

Oh! says the jacket, we shall be drowned;
No, says the petticoat, we shall be found,
We shall be found, we shall be found,
No, says the petticoat, we shall be found.

A miller passed by, and they gave a loud shout,
He put in his hand and he pulled them both out,
Pulled them both out, pulled them both out,
He put in his hand and he pulled them both out.

(Undated)

The beginning's wrong, the end's wrong, but the middle's right. The beginning and the end are about a real well. The middle is about love's well.

A real well doesn't explain anything, even in real terms. But love's well explains everything very well indeed, in love's terms.

Beginning with a real well is wrong because a pig-sty doesn't have a well in it, or by it. Nor would anyone hang clothes to dry by a pig-sty. Second, it is not a *child*'s petticoat that is hanging there, for this petticoat goes with the lad's jacket. So, it must be a girl's petticoat.

After that wrong beginning comes the part that's right. The lad takes off his jacket and hangs it close by the petticoat. Yet his jacket isn't wet. The realistic beginning cannot lead into this part of the rhyme. The lad takes off his jacket and puts it by the petticoat as a sign that he likes to bear a girl company. It's like putting his trousers near her knickers.

The wind blew high, and the clothes fell into the well. That's right, as long as we are taking the wind and the well as signs, too. The wind is the wind of passion. It rises because the two garments have been put together. Otherwise, there is no reason for a real wind starting to blow.

It blows lad and girl into sex, into love's well. How can we know that that meaning's right and that the other meaning – the two pieces of washing blown by bad luck into a well – is wrong? Real washing doesn't talk.

A well comes to be a woman, because it's a round, long, dark hole with water at the bottom. In a similar way, a trap comes to be a mouth, a nut comes to be a head.

The lad, unused to the well, thinks they'll be drowned. The girl has more hope. She knows the well.

The last verse tries to misrepresent what has happened. It was too sexual. So this miller happens along and pulls out both babies with one hand. What a fairy-tale ending! But false, because this miller isn't doing his job. His job is grinding seed, with his rolling stones. But not here. Here, he's just anyone.

So we can reject the last verse. And we can work out what the real ending was. If lad and girl fell into love's well together, a baby got born. It still does, but later than it used to. A child's petticoat would soon be seen, hung out to dry. That right ending suggested the wrong beginning.

The Jerkin and the Petticoat

(Restored)

Man: As I went by my little cow-stall,
          I saw a girl's petticoat hung on the wall.

Chorus Hung on the wall, hung on the wall,
    I saw a girl's petticoat hung on the wall.

Man: I took off my jerkin and hung it near by,
    To bear that petticoat close company.
Chorus: Close company, close company,
    To bear that petticoat close company.

Man: The wind it blew high and down they both fell,
    Jerkin and petticoat into a well.
Chorus: Into a well, into a well,
    Jerkin and petticoat into a well.

Man: 'Oh!' says the jerkin. 'We shall be drowned!'
    'No!' says the petticoat. 'A new world I've found!'
Chorus: 'A new world I've found! New world I've found!'
    'No!' says the petticoat. 'A new world I've found!'

Man: As I went by my little cow-stall,
    I saw a child's petticoat hung on the wall.
Chorus: Hung on the wall, hung on the wall,
    I saw a child's petticoat hung on the wall.

The Wheelbarrow
No. 71, ODNR

When I was a little boy I lived by myself,
And all the bread and cheese I got I laid upon a shelf;
The rats and the mice they made such a strife
I had to go to London town and buy me a wife.

The streets were so broad and the lanes were so narrow,
I was forced to bring my wife home in a wheelbarrow.
The wheelbarrow broke and my wife had a fall,
Farewell wheelbarrow, little wife and all.   (1744)

OTHER VERSIONS:

When I was a wee thing
And just like an elf,
A' the meat that e'er I gat
I laid upon the shelf.
The *rottens* and the mice   [rats]
They fell into a strife,
They wadnae let my meat alane,
Till I gat a wife.

And when I gat a wife,
She wadna bide therein,
Till I gat a *hurl-barrow*   [wheel-barrow]
To hurl her out and in:
The hurl-barrow brake,
My wife she gat a fa',
And the *foul fa'* the hurl-barrow,   [bad luck to]
Cripple wife and a'.

She wadnae eat nae bacon,
She wadnae eat nae beef,
She wadnae eat nae lang kale
For *fyling* o' her teeth,   [defiling?]
But she wad eat the bonie bird,
That sits upon the tree:
Gang down the burn, Davie love,
And I sall follow thee.   (1776)

103

In another version, the first line is given as:

When I was a bachelor …

(1790)

These verses were sung to the tune of 'John Anderson, My Jo' by Robert Burns.

This is the story of someone who could not delve and dig his wife, as Little Dicky did. His wheelbarrow broke. He let his wife down. It was good-bye to her, and bad luck to it.*

When he was a little boy – a bachelor – he lived alone. All his young man's meat he put aside. But rats and mice gave him so much trouble he had to get a wife, to be rid of them. What carnivores are these? Married women and girls, seeking the bachelor's mutton.

He has to bring his wife home, or keep her there, with this wheelbarrow, which 'hurls her out and in'. But it broke, and the Scotch wife wouldn't eat bacon, beef or kale. She wanted the 'bonie bird/That sits upon the tree'. Bonie bird or bonny bird? There's only one bonie, bonny bird that sits on the top of the tree, and that's the cock. He sits on all high places.

The meaning is made doubly clear. The wheelbarrow equals the cock. The cock equals the wheelbarrow.

The last two lines –

Gang down the burn, Davie love
And I sall follow thee'

do not make an end to this story – except to imply that it is about love. The original lines have been changed, to change what the man wanted to say.

But too late. It's already clear what this unhappy husband has to tell. His wife wants loving, or she won't stay home. He must give her the bonie bird.

By putting the song right, we help to put the loving right, too. Primitive people would laugh at us for forgetting so prime a truth.

* 'Little Dicky Delve-and-Dig 'Er' was in *Who Really Killed Cock Robin?*

The Wheelbarrow

(Restored. Tune: 'John Anderson, My Jo')

Oh when I was a youngish lad
I lived just by myself,
And all the meat that I did get
I laid upon a shelf.
The kittens and the hungry cats
They made me such a strife,
They wouldn't let my meat alone
Until I found a wife.

And when I got her home, boys,
She wouldn't stay therein,
Until I made a wheelbarrow
To shove my meat all in.
The wheelbarrow it was too weak,
My meat it did let fall,
So farewell to the wheelbarrow
My woeful wife and all!

She wouldn't eat no mutton,
She wouldn't eat no beef,
She wouldn't eat no bacon,
She was so full of grief.
But she would eat the bonny bird
That's meet as meat can be!
So I must mend the wheelbarrow
To bring her back to me.

Peter, Peter, Pumpkin Eater
No. 405, ODNR

Peter, Peter, pumpkin eater,
Had a wife and couldn't keep her;
He put her in a pumpkin shell
And there he kept her very well.

Peter, Peter, pumpkin eater,
Had another, and didn't love her;
Peter learned to read and spell,
And then he loved her very well.

(1825)

The nursery rhyme is the poem of innocence. The poem of experience is made by learning 'to read and spell'. Standardized spelling means no stand for Peter. But once he can spill as he will, his righting becomes cuneiform. 'Then he loved her very well.'

Peter, Peter, Pumpkin Eater
(Restored)

Peter, Peter, pumpkin eater,
Had a wife and couldn't caper,*
He put in her a pump-in-shell,*
And then he kipt* her very well.

Peter, Peter, pump-can-heat-her,
Had another and didn't love her.
Peter learned to redden, spill,
And then he loved her very well.

* 'Pump' is penis, and 'shell' the female counter-part (Partridge's *Dictionary of Slang*). To 'caper' is to skip like a goat; to 'kip' is to sleep with.

106

Mowing a Meadow
The words were collected by the English Folk Dance
and Song Society

One man and his dog,
Went to mow a meadow.
One man and his dog
Went to mow a meadow.

Two man and his dog
Went to mow a meadow.
Two man, one man and his dog,
Went to mow a meadow.

Three man and his dog
Went to mow a meadow.
Three man, two man, one man and his dog,
Went to mow a meadow.

Four man and his dog
Went to mow a meadow
Four man, three man, two man, one man and his dog,
Went to mow a meadow.

[And so all the way till you reach the tenth man:]

Tenth man and his dog,
Went to mow a meadow,
Ten man, ninth man, eighth man, seventh man, six man,
five man, four man, three man, two man, one man and his
dog,
Went to mow a meadow.

OTHER VERSIONS:
From *Partridge's Dictionary*, 'to mow is the verb for
"copulate with". From 16th. century until 19th. century.'
  Robert Burns uses 'Mowing A Meadow' for a song of 'The
Merry Muses Of Caledonia'.

There are several variations of 'One man shall mow *my meadow*' in the EFD and Song Society Library.

I made my way down a footpath in the Lakes. A handful of lads were singing in the lane. It was dusk. Suddenly, in the midst of them, a lad burst out laughing. It was a song about one man, then two man, then three man, all going to mow a meadow. Then came four man, five man and six man. Yet all had one dog – there never was more than one dog. They seemed to follow one another in, and each had a dog. It would make me think, and think again.

What could they have been doing with a sheepdog? A sheepdog, to mow a meadow? Impossible. What sort of dog was this? He must be a dog with an instinctive face! He must be a phallic dog! That was the only sort that could mow a meadow ... in a girl!

In a girl ... for each man, his work was omitted. We do not know how well it was done or how badly. Then we shall need a tenth man. And we shall see how even the tenth man cannot reap it. Its mowing is possible – and yet impossible, for the work is a wonderland!

So that was why the lad burst out laughing, accidentally. He had timed it right, just as the song was sung. I would make one for each man.

Mowing a Meadow
(Restored)

One man and his dog
Went to mow a meadow.
One man and his dog
Went to mow a meadow!
　　　Wow!

The first man started in,
He flung a furious, fast blow.
He cut a swathe and then
His dog slept in a hollow!
　　　Wow!

Two man and his dog
Went to mow a meadow.
Two man, one man, and his dog,
Went to mow a meadow!
   Wow!

Second man took his time,
He thought he'd lay it all low.
He mowed and mowed, but then
Wider grew the meadow!
   Wow!

Three man and his dog
Went to mow a meadow.
Three man, two man, one man, and his dog,
Went to mow a meadow!
   Wow!

Third man's dog was game,
Had worked in many a meadow,
When the evening came
'Twas worked into a shadow!
   Wow!

Four man and his dog
Went to mow a meadow.
Four man, three man, two man, one man, and his dog,
Went to mow a meadow!
   Wow!

Fourth man's dog was old,
Was grey about the muzzle,
It lay when it was called,
Then curled up in a huddle!
   Wow!

Five man and his dog, *etc.*
Fifth man gave a frown,
At a small, brown meadow,
He said he'd get it mown,

But not today, tomorrow!
　　Wow!

Six man and his dog, *etc.*
Sixth man came along,
Said he'd show 'em all how,
He worked there hard and long,
But hay rose on the meadow!
　　Wow!

Seven man and his dog, *etc.*
Seventh man's dog was young,
Its nose reached to his elbow,
He stayed there all day long,
But his pointer ploughed a furrow!
　　Wow!

Eight man and his dog, *etc.*
Eighth man's dog was lame,
It crept in with its head low,
It slunk away in shame,
He couldn't start the hay-mow!
　　Wow!

Nine man and his dog, *etc.*
Ninth man he strolled by,
Was only casual labour,
He gave it half a try,
But didn't mow that meadow!
　　Wow!

Ten man and his dog, *etc.*
Tenth man mowed away,
A husband and a hero,
His dog played in the hay,
But he didn't mow the meadow!
　　Wow!

All men and their dog
Go to mow a meadow,
All man, each man, that man, this man and his dog,
Cannot mow that meadow!

110

The Old Man
No. 293, ODNR

There was a lady all skin and bone,
Sure such a lady was never known;
It happened upon a certain day,
This lady went to church to pray.

When she came to the church stile,
There she did rest a little while;
When she came to the church yard,
There the bells so loud she heard.

When she came to the church door,
She stopped to rest a little more;
When she came the church within
The parson prayed 'gainst pride and sin.

On looking up, on looking down,
She saw a dead man on the ground;
And from his nose unto his chin,
The worms crawled out, the worms crawled in.

Then she unto the parson said,
Shall I be so when I am dead?
Oh yes! O yes, the parson said,
You will be so when you are dead.

(1810)

If such a lady was never known, she's symbolic, not realistic.
And all her doings likewise.

The nursery rhyme tries to pretend it's about the real
doings of a real lady going to a real church. It does not follow
its own direction: 'Sure, such a lady was never known.' The
result is that all her actions are happenings without any cause.
She rests at the stile, hears the bells, rests a little more at the
church door, sees the dead man and, it's a long horror story, a
nightmare.

We must try to understand, in a different way, the never-known visit this strange figure is making. The most striking event is the finding of the dead man, with worms crawling from his nose to his chin – from apertures, only. This dead man, lying on the ground, with things crawling between nose and chin, is not a rotting corpse but a symbol. It is the climax of that strange church-going.

'I went into the woods/And built me a kirk,' said the girl in 'The Little Coat', earlier. A kirk is a church. What she built was the meeting-place of love. Any big building can symbolize the vagina. It's called a white hall in one rhyme, a barn in another. 'The palace of entrails' was its description thousands of years ago! (*Primitive Erotic Art*, ed. Philip Rawson.)

After a visit to that palace, hall, church, cave, dome, you do find a dead man on the ground, but it's semen that's coming from mouth and chin.

It has to be a male symbol that visits that first church and dies. Instead of a lady finding a dead man, we need some person finding the spent phallus.

Not only does the sense need the change. The verse does too. 'There was a lady all skin and bone' does not scan. There's one syllable too many. And it's in that very word 'lady'. But 'There was a man all skin and bone' does scan.

The seeing eye needs the change. For a lady all skin and bone is just a skinny lady. But a man all skin and bone I have actually seen. He was a curved carving from Easter Island. His head was a knob. His ribs curved round him. His legs were elongated. With mouth open, he was image of the long, round, spuming phallus. 'The man all skin and bone' – the 'bone' has been used before to mean erection. The skin fits.

Here we have a poem about the physical changes experienced by a man during sexual intercourse. The poem must have been told to adolescent boys, who needed to know what happened. It must have been part of some initiation teaching rooted in pre-Christian custom. I predict that there are European rhymes similar to it yet to be found – by a different type of collector.

From old Europe, from a twelfth-century beehive, I saw that the 'worms' should have been 'bees', for the hive had been carved in the shape of a woman, and its entrance was through a hole in the middle of her skirt.

Those responsible for this nursery rhyme did what many missionaries have done. They chopped off the man's sex. They preferred to terrify children with a corpse rather than tell the sexual truth.

That is our background. That is the repression we have to rid our minds of, now, as we read.

The Old Man

(Restored)

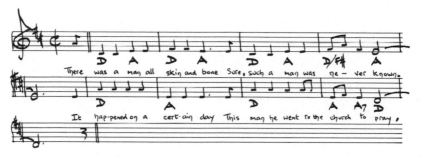

There was a man all skin and bone,
Sure, such a man was never known.
It happened on a certain day
This man he went to church to pray.

When he came to the church-stile,
There he did rest a little while.
When he came to the church-yard,
There he breathed a little hard.

When he came to the church-door,
He stopped to rest a little more.
When he stood the church within,
There he prayed with bone and skin.

He bowed up, and he bowed down.
He fell to an Old Man on the ground;
And from his nose unto his chin,
Bees crawled out, and bees crawled in.

A person to the Old man said
'Are you now for ever dead?'
'Oh no! Oh no!' the Old Man said,
'I come alive when a babe's wanted.'

Carols

Introduction

Two subjects strike my mind. First, that the Church is death-like. I go inside a church, and the corpse-like suffering of Jesus affects me. Mary has a child. But she, alone, has it as a virgin. You can see the unhappiness and the handing-over of himself in Jesus's vocation. This is the anguish of our Sunday, not the joyous reality of Sun Day.

Second, a taxi-driver told me that the priests said that when the Easter coloured eggs were being rolled down the hill and broken, that meant that the stones of Jesus's tomb were being moved. It was a pity that they told such lies. The eggs are broken as a sign of new life, coming for everyone.

I want to restore a Church of Life, not a Church of Death. I want the Yule songs, and the Easter carols. I want to see Eastra, the Goddess of Spring, restored to our world. We have need of her. I want to see a happy man, who shall be married, then leading the celebration.

In AD 600 the Christian priest first began to conquer the Anglo-Saxon gods. By arms, of course. The priest could not change the days of the week – Woden's Day (Wednesday) and, of course, Sun Day – but he deceived us by getting the folk-song tunes introduced with the Mass Book, with Christian words. The clerics were the only ones who could write. They also would punish anyone who broke their law.

The Red Book Of Ossory keeps sixty pagan songs, by the Bishop of Ossory, their tunes arranged for their new Christian songs. They have the old words written over sixteen of them.

Franciscan monks began to change the old pagan beliefs. Yule songs had been about the Yule-time beginning. They had to popularize the story of the Christian Nativity. They wrote that the Three Wise Men called with presents for the child. Who were these Three Wise Men? 25 December was the first day chosen by the pagan Emperor Hadrian (AD 274) to celebrate the birth of the sun. What's more, it must have been that a birth of ever-present man should be born with the sun! He would receive 'The Three Presents', necessary for our marriage and our children.

Christianity has no customs. There is not a custom for birth, marriage or death. But the Church has adopted these old ceremonies. Where do the holly and the ivy come from? Where does the decoration in our houses come from, to banish our darkness? The presents of Yule Tide Day, the lights and the fire, the giving of holly and ivy to the dead, are all customs from the Anglo-Saxon past. You can look up 'Christmas' in the *Encyclopaedia Britannica*.

'Wassail' does mean 'Be in health', but it also means 'Good health', as we wish our friends in a pub. The mistletoe, the ever-present Yule follower, is always with us. People are still able to kiss beneath it. The cock was always on the steeple. Why, no one now knows; but they knew 500 years ago. Till 1350, the phallus was still displayed, and then hidden, in the altar.* In church carvings we can see the Greenery of the World, and the Green Man, amongst us. They are still with us! Yule songs were in the fourteenth century described as '*obscenus, turpis, indecens, diabolicus*', all from the carols which the priests hated. And so they changed them.

The Christian carol is a contradiction. A Yule carol will

---

* Professor Webb, quoted in the *Roots Of Witchcraft* by Michael Harrison (Muller, 1973).

equal its popularity with the past, for the unconquerability is again to be celebrated. There should not be a mark of weakness, or of suffering, in the on-going of the year. Priests are waiting for the tragic Good Friday.

'Paganism' is an old word. You may not connect dancing with paganism. Yet it happened on Saturn's Day (Saturday) and will always excite men and women. Decorating a beautiful thing with flowers does not strike you as being pagan. Yet there it is, from decorating a wedding to standing a pot of flowers on a grave.

There is a pagan stone inside St Peter's Church at Heysham, Lancashire. It has Yggdrasil, the Tree of Life, engraved on it. It has animals with huge tails, and a man with hands, holding up Heaven. Each side of them is a mythical, double-headed animal. Such a sign is more compulsive, and more effective, than anything written down later on. They are symbols of life going on. They will instruct us, as science will advance us. As astronomy encourages us to think scientifically, so these songs shall summon Yule, the time immemorable of every man.

Yule Wassails and Carols

The Gloucestershire Wassail
No. 31, OBC*

Wassail, wassail, all over the town!
Our toast it is white, and our ale it is brown,
Our bowl it is made of the white maple tree;
With the wassailing bowl we'll drink to thee.

So here is to Cherry and to his right cheek,
Pray God send our master a good piece of beef,
And a good piece of beef that may we all see;
With the wassailing bowl we'll drink to thee.

And here is to Dobbin and to his right eye,
Pray God send our master a good Christmas pie,
And a good Christmas pie that may we all see;
With our wassailing bowl we'll drink to thee.

So here is to Broad May and to her broad horn,
May God send our master a good crop of corn,
And a good crop of corn that may we all see;
With the wassailing bowl we'll drink to thee.

And here is to Fillpail and to her left ear,
Pray God send our master a happy New Year,
And a happy New Year as e'er he did see;
With our wassailing bowl we'll drink to thee.

And here is to Colly and to her long tail,
Pray God send our master he never may fail
A bowl of strong beer; I pray you draw near,
And our jolly wassail it's then you shall hear.

Come, butler, come fill us a bowl of the best,
Then we hope that your soul in heaven may rest;

* OBC = The Oxford Book of Carols.

But if you do draw us a bowl of the small,
Then down shall go butler, bowl and all.

Then here's to the maid in the lily white smock,
Who tripped to the door and slipped back the lock!
Who tripped to the door and pulled back the pin,
For to let these jolly wassailers in.

Did our ancestors sing such nonsense? Or has the song become senile? 'Our toast it is white.' White toast? 'Come, butler.' Butler? Jeeves? Where are we? What's going on?

We're going round a farm, singing. In Somerset, they sing to the people (as in 'The May-Pluckers Carol'*). In Gloucestershire, we sing to the horses and cows! Why? Because Wassail means 'Be healthy'. We – Norse – want healthy stock, healthy crops, healthy people.

So here is to Cherry and to his right cheek
Pray God send our master a good piece of beef.

We didn't always sing rubbish. We used to be able to rhyme. We've become poor – poor farm labourers. And we're begging. We want beef. And we've changed whatever was there into insignificance. I wish it were a right piece of cheek – that would have been a more jolly Wassail.

If we took out that beggarly rhyme, what would we have? 'So here is to Cherry ... Pray God send our master ...' What was in the gaps?

Let's read on regardless, through Dobbin and his right eye (to rhyme with 'pie') and we shall come to Broad May. At least she's got a broad horn. And 'May God send our master a good crop of corn' isn't begging. It is a healthy wish. The horn is a more significant part of the animal, too. So here's a less altered verse, one easier to restore.

We'd be all right if we could understand why the animal's called Broad May. What's in a name? Meaning! Cherry, Dobbin, Fillpail, Colly – all meaningful. But, Broad May?

So let's work out who this is. Cherry and Dobbin are horses. Fillpail's the cow. So Broad May is the bull. It used to be called Barney! Hence his broad horn.

Now we've got the pattern of the verses. An important

122

animal, an important part and then an important crop.

More than that, the animals are in pairs. Cherry and Dobbin weren't just horses. They were mare and stallion. We have to find important parts of them that rhyme with main farm crops.

Then comes Colly, with her long tail. Now Colly isn't a third cow – as the editor of the OBC says it is. Even two cows were one too many! Is Colly a cow's name? With a long tail? Colly used to be a dog when I lived in Gloucestershire.

His long tail is his important part, and one with a significance that could lead on to the master's own seed-crop not failing. This dog is the same one as the 'girt dog of Devonport who burned his long tail', in 'The Warm Wassail' – for the Somerset lads.

It isn't only poverty that's got us farm-labourers down. It's sexual repression. Thomas Hardy wrote books about it. So we had to call the dog 'her' to disguise his sexuality. We've done the same with Broad May.

The butler and the Christian wish can vanish with the toast. In their servile place, we should put 'the mistress' to go with the master. And, to fit 'in heaven may rest', in a Wassail sense, when our master doesn't fail.

The maid and her lily-white tits – sorry, 'smock' – are out. We've well-wished the animals and crops, then the master and mistress. If we go on to the maid, we'll have to go on to the son. We'll be singing the Somersetshire 'Warm Wassail'!* The 'Farm Wassail' must have to stick to the farm. The lily-white 'smock' was only to pull back the 'lock' and get hungry wassailers in to the farmhouse.

We don't care if we stay outside. We've got the Wassail bowl out here. We've been singing 'We'll drink to thee' at the end of every verse. So we need a drinking chorus. I heard the Watersons sing a 'Fol-de-dol' one, in their version on record. But a meaningful song needs a meaningful chorus. And the meaning is plain enough. 'Come, landlord, fill the flowing bowl until it doth run over' – only our Wassail bowl was bigger than a punch bowl and was 'dressed up with garlands and ribbons' in Gloucestershire, in 1868. The bowl had kept its beauty and its hidden meaning.

* 'The May-Pluckers Carol' and 'The Warm Wassail' are in *Who Really Killed Cock Robin?*

123

The Farm Wassail

(Restored)

We wassail our way all over the town,
Our bowl it is white and our ale it is brown,
Our bowl it is made of the good apple-tree,
With our wassailing bowl we'll drink unto ye.

Chorus:
Fill the bowl, fill the bowl so full, fill the bowl so fair, fill
the bowl so free,
Fill it flowing, fill it over, Now – drink round with we!

To Dobbin the horse, and to his strong thigh,
May God send our neighbour a strong crop of hay,
A strong crop of hay, that we shall all see,
With our wassailing bowl we'll drink unto ye.
Chorus:

To Cherry the mare, and to her thick coat,
May God send our neighbour a thick crop of oat,
A thick crop of oat, that we shall all see,
With our wassailing bowl we'll drink unto ye.
Chorus:

To Barney the bull, and to his big horn,
May God send our neighbour a big crop of corn,
A big crop of corn, that we shall all see,
With our wassailing bowl we'll drink unto ye.
Chorus:

To Fillpail the cow, and to her full teat,
May God send our neighbour a full crop of wheat,
A full crop of wheat, that we shall all see,
With our wassailing bowl we'll drink unto ye.
Chorus:

To Colly the dog, and to his long tail,
May God send our neighbour that he does not fail,

He long does not fail, that we shall all see,
With our wassailing bowl we'll drink unto ye.
Chorus:

Come neighbour, come fill our bowl with the best,
May God send our neighbour a best night of rest,
A best night of rest, that we shall all see,
With our wassailing bowl we'll drink unto ye.

Chorus:
Fill the bowl, fill the bowl so full, fill the bowl so fair, fill
the bowl so free
Fill it flowing, fill it over, Now – drink round with we!

Buff Blow

English Dance and Song magazine (published English Folk Dance and Song Society)

Buff blow, Farewell,
God send you 'ere well,
Every sprig and every spray,
A bushel of apples to give away,
On New Year's Day in the morning,
Shoo'ee.

Buff blow, Farewell,
God send you 'ere well,
Apples to roast, nuts to crack,
A barrel of cider ready to tap,
On New Year's Day in the morning,
Shoo'ee.

The old year's out,
The new year's in,
Please open the door,
And let us in,
On New Year's Day in the morning,
Shoo'ee.

There is a Wassail collected as late as 1980 by Gwylim and Carol Davies in Cheltenham. It is amazing how Wassails survive, but through Christianity and respectability these pagan fertility songs still persist.

They have suffered, though. Old-fashioned words are misunderstood, or misheard; and old-fashioned ideas are often censored – sometimes by the singers themselves, since, traditionally, they are poor people singing to wealthier ones. The parson, too, might also get to hear ... So we are left with not a Wassail but what is left of one. By thinking about the words, though, it is still possible to guess at the uncensored ones.

126

What does the first line mean? 'Farewell' cannot mean 'goodbye', for the singers have only just come! So, it must mean 'prosper well'. Second, 'Buff' cannot mean 'buffet', or there would be two blows. So, how about 'bare skin' (*Chambers Dictionary*)? 'Give me a blow in your bare skin, and prosper well!' That is a good start for a Wassail, as confetti is for a wedding.

'God send you ere well' must follow on. Not 'God send you ever well' but 'God send you bear well', for then the lines about 'every sprig and every spray' shall have their verb about bearing.

And the 'Shoo'ee'? As we are not scaring crows, it must be 'surely' to fit with New Year's Day.

The second verse begins with the same 'bare skin' blow and continues, as it should, with plenty of everything – apples, nuts and cider. But the third verse has lost its striking start, the 'buff blow'. And when it is put back, there are too many lines for one stanza. We must therefore conclude that there were two verses which have been forced into one, with only the respectable lines kept. All verse 3 says now is 'Please let us in'; there is not much to sing about there!

And how does 'The old year's out, the new year's in' come to fit a fertility song? We have a naked couple; we have cider; and we have 'surely'. Surely it must be time to get up now? Surely it is time to put some clothes on ...

Let us modernize the language. Fertility cannot die, after all. So while love is always old-fashioned, its current songs never are.

The 'Love Naked and Long' Wassail

(Restored)

Love naked and long,
Kids healthy and strong,
Here's holly sprig, here's ivy spray,
A bunch of mistletoe leads the way,
On New Year's Day in the morning,
Surely!

Love naked and long,
Kids healthy and strong,
Apples to roast, walnuts to crack,
A barrel of scrumpy ready to tap,
On New Year's Day in the morning,
Surely!

Love naked and long,
Kids healthy and strong,
The Old Year is out, the New Year is in,
And may you both be in your skin,
On New Year's Day in the morning,
Surely!

Love naked and long,
Kids healthy and strong,
Get you up now, open the door,
It's time to let in a good neighbour,
On New Year's Day in the morning,
Surely!

Love nak-ed and long, Kids health-y and strong, Here's holly sprig,

Here's ivy spray, A bunch of mistletoe leads the way, On New Years day in the

morn- ing, Sure-ly! [The original "Buff Blow" was in ¾ time]

The Twelve Days of Christmas
(ed.) R. Nettal, *Carols, 1400-1950*

On the twelfth day of Christmas
My true love sent to me
Twelve lords a-leaping,
Eleven ladies dancing,
Ten pipers playing,
Nine drummers drumming,
Eight maids a-milking,
Seven swans a-swimming,
Six geese a-laying,
Five gold rings,
Four colly birds,
Three French hens,
Two turtle doves
And a partridge in a pear tree.

[Note: This is the last verse. The carol proceeds day by day, adding a new gift to those already given.]

OTHER VERSIONS:
Verses 6 and 7 of No. 136 in *The Early English Carols* are:

Holly has birds, a full fair flock,
The nightingale, the poppingay, the gentle laverock.
Good ivy, what birds hast thou?
None but the owlet that cries 'How, how!'

There was only one word of Christian indoctrination in the carol, and I took that out of the title. But there has been much loss of meaning. The gifts don't make sense.

The chorus keeps telling us 'My true love sent to me'. So, all these gifts must be love-gifts. We have to rediscover the 'language of birds'. There is a 'language of flowers', which we still remember because flowers are still sent by lovers to each other. If, on the first day, my true love sent a violet, and on the twelfth day he sent a red rose, we would be able to guess his meaning.

The verses in the other versions show that language being used. Holly has the male birds. Ivy has the only female one, the owlet who cries 'Ooo! Ooo!' – in the woods, at night. Here, the bird symbols have been partially lost. After the swans a-swimming, human beings replace them. But they are not Christian saints, only secular maids, drummers, pipers, ladies and lords. They are roughly equivalent to the birds they replaced. The playing and drumming, the dancing and leaping, do make a partial climax to all the presents. If we can find the bird symbols that were sent originally, we shall restore the full climax.

The form of the song helps us to do that, for the end is the same as the beginning. The singers reach the twelfth gift and then sing their way back to the first. The song is circular, and the climax joins the overture. Lords a-leaping, and the partridge in the pear tree, go together.

The pear tree, because of the shape of pears and their softness and sweetness and their juice, is an image of woman. The partridge has red legs. That one detail has been enough for him to be chosen as a male symbol. The red breast of the robin is equally sufficient. A red-legged bird in a Garden of Eden pear tree … the lover sends his full message even in his first gift. But it's a picture, an image. The last gift is an action.

That action can be deduced. It is male. The lords do it, while the ladies dance. It is the climax of love. Twelve cocks a-crowing, eleven hens a-crooning.

The link between actions and pictures is 'six geese a-laying'. It means laying down, not laying eggs. True loves prefer the one to the other.

Now we have understood the message of the gifts, we can see through the other numbers. Two turtle doves are twins. They are white and soft. The three French hens are wrong. The 'French' was meant to convey sexual associations – which may tell us when the alteration was made. Three French cocks would be better, only no such birds exist! The four 'colly birds' were four coal-ly birds, because coal black was the colour of sexual sin. Hence, the Black Bull. 'Five gold rings' was someone's desire to get this couple married quick, before the

130

action started. They should, of course, be birds.

Once the actions start, their form limits our choice of bird. They have to be in pairs, like pipers and drummers, and their names have to alliterate with their actions, like 'maids a-milking'. All the actions have to lead to the 'twelve cocks a-crowing'. But now we know where we're going, and who is going with us, we can find them. The 'French hens', the 'gold rings', the 'ladies dancing', hid the beauty and the power of the image of the partridge in the pear tree.

The Twelve Days of New Year
(Restored)

On the first day of New Year
My true love sent to me
A partridge in a pear tree.

On the second day of New Year
My true love sent to me
Two turtle doves
And a partridge in a pear tree.

On the third day of New Year
My true love sent to me
Three missel-cocks,
Two turtle doves
And a partridge in a pear tree.

On the fourth day of New Year
My true love sent to me
Four bunting birds, *etc.*

On the fifth day of New Year
My true love sent to me
Five nestlings, *etc.*

On the sixth day of New Year
My true love sent to me
Six wrens a-laying, *etc.*

On the seventh day of New Year
My true love sent to me
Seven robins rising, *etc.*

On the eighth day of New Year
My true love sent to me
Eight swifts a-swooping, *etc.*

On the ninth day of New Year
My true love sent to me
Nine ducks a-dipping, *etc.*

On the tenth day of New Year
My true love sent to me
Ten drakes a-diving, *etc.*

On the eleventh day of New Year
My true love sent to me
Eleven hens a-crooning, *etc.*

On the twelfth day of New Year
My true love sent to me
Twelve cocks a-crowing,
Eleven hens a-crooning,
Ten drakes a-diving,
Nine ducks a-dipping,
Eight swifts a-swooping,
Seven robins rising,
Six wrens a-laying,
Five nestlings,
Four bunting birds,
Three missel cocks,
Two turtle doves
And a partridge in a pear tree.

A Gaping Wide-Mouthed Waddling Frog

No. 176, ODNR

A gaping wide-mouthed waddling frog.

Two pudding ends would choke a dog,
With a gaping wide-mouthed waddling frog.

Three monkeys tied to a clog,
Two pudding ends would choke a dog,
With a gaping wide-mouthed waddling frog.

Four horses stuck in a bog,
Three monkeys tied to a clog
Two pudding ends would choke a dog,
With a gaping wide-mouthed waddling frog.

Five puppies by our dog, Ball,
Who daily for their breakfast call;
Four horses stuck in a bog,
Three monkeys tied to a clog, *etc.*

Six beetles against a wall,
Close by an old woman's apple-stall;
Five puppies by our dog, Ball, *etc.*

Seven lobsters in a dish,
As fresh as any heart could wish;
Six beetles against a wall, *etc.*

Eight joiners in joiner's hall,
Working with their tools and all;
Seven lobsters in a dish, *etc.*

Nine peacocks in the air,
I wonder how they all came there,

I don't know, nor I don't care;
Eight joiners in joiner's hall, *etc.*

Ten comets in the sky,
Some low and some high;
Nine peacocks in the air, *etc.*

Eleven ships sailing o'er the main,
Some bound for France and some for Spain;
Ten comets in the sky, *etc.*

Twelve huntsmen with horns and hounds,
Hunting over other men's grounds;
Eleven ships sailing o'er the main,
Some bound for France and some for Spain;
Ten comets in the sky,
Some low and some high;
Nine peacocks in the air,
I wonder how they all came there,
I don't know, nor I don't care;
Eight joiners in joiner's hall,
Working with their tools and all;
Seven lobsters in a dish,
As fresh as any heart could wish;
Six beetles against a wall,
Close by an old woman's apple-stall;
Five puppies by our dog, Ball,
Who daily for their breakfast call;
Four horses stuck in a bog,
Three monkeys tied to a clog,
Two pudding ends would choke a dog,
With a gaping, wide-mouthed waddling frog.

'It was popular, especially at Christmas time, up to the middle of the 19th century, Eckenstein compares the rhyme with "The Twelve Days of Christmas" '. ODNR.

'The Twelve Days of Christmas' must have been too genteel for some peasant. That 'partridge in a pear tree' must have been too remote from what his true love sent to him. So he made a crude version, as the revenge of realism.

His low-life truth was censored when it was printed in 1760. Then its popularity slowly died. By the middle of the nineteenth century, the rhyme was no longer said. Today it's no longer even read or understood. 'It is unlikely that there is any special significance in the imagery,' writes the editor of the ODNR.

I have to open the reader's mind, so he visualizes the specific significance.

A gaping, wide-mouthed, waddling frog ... not a real frog ... the stress is on the '*gaping, wide*-mouthed *waddling* frog.' Why are frogs still made in brass, as ornaments? Why do the French call prostitutes 'frogs'? (The reference is found in Jean Renoir's biography of his father Pierre Renoir.) Why is it, in a nursery rhyme, that it is a frog who would a-wooing go?

Frogs have big back legs that are far apart. Frogs have loose, slack mouths, without teeth. Frogs waddle. Frogs are fat, soft and slippery. A gaping, wide-mouthed, waddling frog is a woman image. The brass ornaments are old fertility signs. The frog would go a-wooing because girls would, and might, meet a rat. Frogs jump.

The pudding ends? Round puddings with the ends tied up into a little frill go with the frog. Puddings are breasts; the ends, tits. 'Two turtle doves' in 'The Twelve Days' followed the 'partridge in the pear tree'.

The three monkeys are monkeying, with a clog that is a debased shoe, a slipper, a sign of woman. Clogs fit de-standardized feet. The four horses are stuck down there, in a bog. The puppies are calling for their supper, every night, or for their breakfast, every morning. They're by the big dog, Ball – which names its predecessors.

Those beetles aren't little black insects in the kitchen. They're the great, soft mallets used to lay paving stones. They're bashing with their soft-hard heads at a wall, by the place where a woman stalls apples. Lobsters are red, their great claws clawing. I don't even have to explain any more! The joiners with their tools are joining in the joiner's hall. And the peacocks, with their omitted tails in the air. The comets, some low and some high! Down and up is a good motion! What furrows there are in that main! The sea is the oldest image of woman, and that's where the name Mary comes from! And the huntsmen hunting over other men's grounds chase other men's wives.

Once repression's gone, crude life returns. The rhyme's 'special significance' is seen. But, but ... that isn't restoring the rhyme as a carol. For, like Eckenstein, I am sure this is a 'The Twelve Nights of New Year'. The number, the way the verse builds up and repeats, the subject-matter, are the same. But to refit the rhyme's words to the tune is difficult. I have to go far from the rhyme – while keeping in touch with it. It's a long journey back through time to the base. Back to base life. There is no base life. Back to life ...

> Someone behind drinks ale,
> And opens mussels, and croaks scraps of songs
> Towards the ham-hung rafters about love.
> Dick deals the cards. Wet, century-wide trees
> Clash in surrounding starlessness above
> This lamplit cave, where Jan turns back and farts,
> Gobs at the grate, and hits the queen of hearts.
> Rain, wind, and fire! The secret, bestial peace!
> 'The Card Players', Philip Larkin

At last Philip Larkin and I meet in 'Scraps of Songs' about love. We have been going round the world, in opposite directions, ever since we left college at the same time. Now we meet. But he's left his remark, 'the secret, bestial peace' of the creative place. I've come to it via the South Sea Islands and find his Black Flag flying at the Pole.

With a Gaping, Wide-Mouthed, Waddling Frog
(Restored)

With a gaping, wide-mouthed, waddling frog.

Two pudding-ends would choke a dog,
With a gaping, wide-mouthed, waddling frog.

Three monkeys monkeying with a clog,
Two pudding-ends would choke a dog,
With a gaping, wide-mouthed, waddling frog.

Four horses stuck fast in a bog,
Three monkeys monkeying with a clog,
Two pudding-ends would choke a dog,
With a gaping, wide-mouthed, waddling frog.

[It goes on, until you meet the last verse]

Twelve horsemen with their horn and hounds,
Hunting over other men's grounds.
Eleven ships ploughing up the main,
Some come from France, some come from Spain.
Ten comets blazing in the sky,
They blaze down low, they blaze up high.
Nine peacocks with their tails in air,
I wonder how they all got there?
Eight joiners in an open hall,
Working with their tools and all.
Seven lobsters in a dainty dish,
As fresh and red as heart could wish.
Six picks swinging at a wall,
That fronts a woman's apple-stall.
Five pups, near the bull-dog Ball,
Who nightly for their supper call.
Four horses stuck fast in a bog,
Three monkeys monkeying with a clog,
Two pudding-ends would choke a dog,
With a gaping, wide-mouthed, waddling frog.

The Twelve Nights of New Year

(Restored. Tune, 'The Twelve Days of Christmas')

On the first night of New Year
My old girl sent to me
A ruby in a froggie.

On the second night of New Year
My old girl sent to me
Two suet puds
And a ruby in a froggie.

On the third night of New Year
My old girl sent to me
Three monkey-nuts,
Two suet puds
And a ruby in a froggie.

On the fourth night of New Year
My old girl sent to me
Four rosy hips,
Three monkey-nuts,
Two suet puds, *etc.*

On the fifth night of New Year
My old girl sent to me
Five ball-rooms,
Four rosy hips, *etc.*

On the sixth night of New Year
My old girl sent to me
Six picks a-picking,
Five ball-rooms, *etc.*

On the seventh night of New Year
My old girl sent to me
Seven lobsters lobbing,
Six picks a-picking, *etc.*

On the eighth night of New Year
My old girl sent to me
Eight joiners joining,
Seven lobsters lobbing, *etc.*

On the ninth night of New Year
My old girl sent to me
Nine peacocks pointing,
Eight joiners joining, *etc.*

On the tenth night of New Year
My old girl sent to me
Ten comets coming,
Nine peacocks pointing, *etc.*

On the eleventh night of New Year
My old girl sent to me
Eleven mummies mumming,
Ten comets coming, *etc.*

On the twelfth night of New Year
My old girl sent to me
Twelve horsemen hunting,
Eleven mummies mumming,
Ten comets coming,
Nine peacocks pointing,
Eight joiners joining,
Seven lobsters lobbing,
Six picks a-picking,
Five ball-rooms,
Four rosy hips,
Three monkey-nuts,
Two suet puds
And a ruby in a froggie.

Patapan
No. 82, OBC

Willie, take your little drum,
With your whistle, Robin, come!
When we hear the fife and drum,
Tu-re-lu-re-lu; pat-a-pat-a-pan,
When we hear the fife and drum,
Christmas should be frolicsome.

Thus the men of olden days
Love the King of kings to praise;
When they hear the fife and drum,
Tu-re-lu-re-lu; pat-a-pat-a-pan,
When they hear the fife and drum,
Sure our children won't be dumb!

God and man are now become
More at one than fife and drum.
When you hear the fife and drum,
Tu-re-lu-re-lu; pat-a-pat-a-pan,
When you hear the fife and drum,
Dance, and make the village hum!

OTHER VERSIONS: PATAPAN (BURGUNDIAN
ORIGINAL)
Guillaume prends ton tambourin,
Toi, prends ta flûte, Robin,
Au son de ces instruments,
Tu re lu re lu; pat a pat a pan,
Au son de ces instruments
Je dirai Noë gaîment.

C'était la mode autrefois
De louer le Roi des rois,
Au son de ces instruments,
Tu re lu re lu; pat a pat a pan,

Au son de ces instruments
Il nous en faut faire autant.

L'homme et Dieu sont plus d'accord
Que la flûte et le tambour;
Au son de ces instruments,
Tu re lu re lu; pat a pat a pan,
Au son de ces instruments
Chantons, dansons, sautons-en.

My translation:
Guillaume, take your tambourine,/You [thou] take your flute, Robin;/At the sound of these instruments/Tu-re-lu-re-lu; pat-a-pat-a-pan,/At the sound of these instruments/I'll say Noel gaily.

It was the custom formerly/To praise the King of kings/At the sound of these instruments,/Tu-re-lu-re-lu; pat-a-pat-a-pan,/At the sound of these instruments/We must do as much.

Man and God are more in accord/Than the flute and the tambourine;/At the sound of these instruments,/Tu-re-lu-re-lu; pat-a-pat-a-pan,/At the sound of these instruments/Let us sing, dance and leap.

If the reader quickly turned away from the silly simplicity of the English carol, he shared my first reaction. But then I looked at the Burgundian original. Flute and drum! Flute and drum! Not 'whistle and little drum'. Give the man, Robin, back his long flute. It's his. And who should have the drum, the rattling drum, the tambourine? I know the Burgundian says Guillaume, but there's only one person who has a round drum. That's Jenny. They're the pair who make music.

There's an English folk-song, 'I'm Seventeen Come Sunday', which uses the musical instruments in a similar symbolic way –

And now she is the soldier's wife
And the soldier loves her dearly,
The drum and fife is her delight
And a merry old man is mine-O!

This is going to be a merry old song!

We're right, because of 'Man and God are more in accord/Than the flute and the tambourine.' For man could be either instrument, but how can God resemble the other? So the monks have been up to their clever-silly work again. 'At the sound of these instruments,/Let us dance, sing, and leap.' That doesn't sound like a hymn, either …

So we can deal with the wrong details, the wrong translation, the misunderstandings. The instruments should play together, not consecutively. The childish 'little drum', 'frolicsome' and 'Willie' can be removed. The Burgundians began to change the song by converting it to praise 'the King of kings'. After that, the Englishman, with his usual bloody-cold (old Burgundian for 'sang froid'), made us fit for the kingdom of heaven, where the little children go.

Here on earth, I found the tune is near 'The Jug of Punch', so I made the words fit that, to make the song at home in its new country.

The Flute and Drum
(Restored: Tune – 'Jug of Punch')

Solo:
Now, Jenny, play on your rounded drum;
Robin, raise your flute to the drum's rhythm;
So to the music of union
I'll cry 'New Year is happ'ly come!'
Chorus, Men:
Tool-a-rool-a-rool, tool-a-rool-a-rool, tool-a-rool-a-rool, tool-a-rool-a-rool.
Chorus, Women:
Bing-a-bang-a-bang, bing-a-bang-a-bang, bing-a-bang-a-bang, bing-a-bang-a-bang.
Together:
So to the music of union
I'll cry 'New Year is happ'ly come!'

Solo:
The men and women of olden days

Played this good old tune for the sun's upraise,
So to the music of union
We must do just what's been always done!
Chorus, Men:
Tool-a-rool-a-rool, tool-a-rool-a-rool, tool-a-rool-a-rool,
tool-a-rool-a-rool.
Chorus, Women:
Bing-a-bang-a-bang, bing-a-bang-a-bang, bing-a-bang-a-
bang, bing-a-bang-a-bang.
Together:
So to the music of union
We must do just what's been always done.

Solo:
A man and wife are still more at one
Than this fleeting flute and this beating drum,
So to the music of union
Let us dance and sing, and together come!
Chorus, Men:
Tool-a-rool-a-rool, tool-a-rool-a-rool, tool-a-rool-a-rool,
tool-a-rool-a-rool.
Chorus, Women:
Bing-a-bang-a-bang, bing-a-bang-a-bang, bing-a-bang-a-
bang, bing-a-bang-a-bang.
Together:
So to the music of union
Let us dance and sing, and together come!

All and Some
No. 62, OBC

Burden:
Nowell sing we both all and some,
Now *Rex pacificus* is y-come.   [peaceful King]

Solo:
Exortum est in love and *lysse*,   [it is risen up; joy]
Now Christ his *gree* he gan us *gysse*   [prize: prepare]
And with his body us brought to bliss.

Burden:
Both all and some, both all and some.

Solo:
De fructu ventris of Mary bright   [of the womb's fruit]
Both God and man in her alight
Out of disease he did us *dight*:   [make ready]

Burden:
Both all and some, both all and some.

Solo:
Puer natus to us was sent,   [a boy born]
To bliss us brought, fro *bale* us *blent*,   [harm; turned aside]
Or else to woe we had *ywent*:   [gone]

Burden:
Both all and some, both all and some.

Solo:
Lux fulgebit with love and light.   [The light will shine]
In Mary mild his pennon *pight*,   [pitched]
In her took *kind* with manly might: [nature]

Burden:
Both all and some, both all and some.

Solo:
Gloria tibi, ay, and bliss,   [glory to thee]
God unto his grace he us *wysse*,   [lead]
The *rent* of heaven that we not miss: [hold]

145

Burden:
Both all and some, both all and some.

Let's lighten the Burden to start with. Instead of 'Now *Rex pacificus* is y-come' let's have 'The Sun Unconquered is come!' For the angels did not say 'Nowell' in the Bible's Nativity story. We shouted 'Nowell!', all of us, for any good news, anything novel, anything being born. It was shouted in London at news of Agincourt. Our cry of joy at the New Year was for the sun's birth. The very next piece of Latin confirms that. '*Exortum est*' means 'It is risen up.' Not even 'He is risen up.' Perhaps this monk thought he couldn't put that for a New Year carol? 'He is risen up' is, of course, for Easter.

Oh Latin, what frauds are committed in thy name! 'The light will shine with love and light.' Once the '*Lux fulgebit*' is translated, how the repetition shows! The monk is relying on people's being unable to translate. 'Thou art Peter, and on this rock I will build my Church.' If people had known this depended on the pun on the Latin word Petrus, they might have wondered, as I now do, if it was Christ who spoke Latin as well as that.

Having removed the hocus-pocus, what is to take its place? The sun. Then, in whom or what did the sun pitch his pennon? In whom or what did he take nature with manly might? In Mother Earth. The 'manly might' is the give-away phrase. Jesus, especially baby Jesus, cannot be referred to as a being of 'manly might'. But it does fit the sun, the supreme male god, beaming on earth, making it fertile again. I see the pennons striking down through the winter clouds.

The Latin of the last verse is just a tag. Anything will do, when only sound is wanted. 'Glory to thee, ay, and bliss.' Happiness cannot be wished to Jesus in heaven. It's like taking coals to Newcastle. The meaningful line is the second, where we are to be guided to some sort of heaven. This guiding follows the insemination of the Earth. Now it's the pitching of our pennon which is to be directed to some sort of happiness.

'The rent of heaven that we not miss.' We have paid it till now. But the lease has just expired.

146

Carol of the Unconquered Sun

(Restored)

Chorus:
Both all and some, both all and some,
Nowell sing we, both all and some,
The Sun Unconquered is now come.

Solo 1:
He's risen up in love and joy,
Flames out his presence from the sky,
His being brings us gaiety,
Chorus:

Solo 2:
Out of the womb of deepest night,
He's sprung with growing warmth and light,
To cure disease, and put us right,
Chorus:

147

Solo 3:
The saving Sun to us was sent,
To bliss us brought, from blackness bent,
Or else to death we down had went,
Chorus:

Solo 4:
Oh, he will shine with love and light,
In fair furrows his pennons strike,
The earth is stirred with manly might,
Chorus:

Solo 5:
Praise to the Sun for our comfort,
He's guided us to join his sport,
We hold our happiness as he has sought.

Chorus:
Both all and some, both all and some,
Nowell sing we, both all and some,
The Sun Unconquered is now come.

A Christmas Song

(Current Version)

The three characters: Nought, New Guise and Now-a-Days
sing:

Now I pray all ye yeomanry that is here
To sing with us with merry cheer.

It is written with a coal   [colle, cole]
It is written with a coal

He that shitteth with his hole   [hoyll]
He that shitteth with his hole

But he wipe his arse clean
But he wipe his arse clean

On his breech it shall be seen.   [breche]
On his breech it shall be seen.

Holyke, Holyke, Holyke!
Holyke, Holyke, Holyke!

This is from *Mankind*, a morality play, *c.* 1450, in *The Macro
Plays* published by Kegan Paul. There is no note, that I could
detect, on 'Holyke, Holyke, Holyke' by Furnivall and
Pollard, the editors. I tried Hole-lick, Hole leak etc.

It shows what was sung by the Jan van Hogspeuw, Dirk
Dogstoerd and Old Prijck. As they live on, in at least two of
us, I gave them a little tune. They remind me of my uncles and
my grandfather and the lavatory-seat with two wooden
covers over the earth-closet.

It reminds me of today.

The Coal-Hole Carol

(Restored)

Solo: It is written with a coal,
Chorus: It is written with a coal,

Solo: He that shitteth with his hole,
Chorus: He that shitteth with his hole,

Solo: Less he wipe his bum-gut clean,
Chorus: Less he wipe his bum-gut clean,

Solo: On his shirt shall it be seen.
Chorus: On his shirt shall it be seen.

Solo: Arsehole, arsehole, arsehole, soul;
Chorus: Arsehole, arsehole, arsehole, soul.

The Angel Gabriel
No. 37, OBC

The angel Gabriel from God
Was sent to Galilee,
Unto a virgin fair and free
Whose name was called Mary.
And when the angel thither came,
He fell down on his knee,
And looking up in the virgin's face,
He said 'All hail, Mary.'

Chorus:
Then sing we all, both great and small,
'Nowell, Nowell, Nowell';
We may rejoice to hear the voice
Of the angel Gabriel.

Mary anon looked him upon,
And said 'Sir, what are ye?
I marvel much at these tidings
Which thou hast brought to me.
Married I am unto an old man,
As the lot fell unto me;
Therefore, I pray, depart away,
For I stand in doubt of thee.'
Chorus:

'Mary,' he said, 'be not afraid,
But do believe in me;
The power of the Holy Ghost
Shall overshadow thee:
Thou shalt conceive without any grief,
As the Lord told unto me:
God's own dear son from heaven shall come,
And shall be born of thee.'
Chorus:

This came to pass as God's will was,
Even as the angel told,
About midnight an angel bright
Came to the shepherds' fold.
And told them then both where and when
Born was the child our Lord,
And all along this was their song,   ·
'All glory be given to God.'
Chorus:

Good people all, both great and small,
The which do hear my voice,
With one accord let's praise the Lord,
And in our hearts rejoice:
Like sister and brother, let's love one another
Whilst we our lives do spend,
Whilst we have space let's pray for grace,
And so let my carol end.
Chorus:

It's been done conscientiously. Reading Luke 1, verses 26 to 35, I found point after point included. Gabriel was sent from God, to Galilee, to a virgin whose name was Mary. When she saw him, she was troubled at his news; and Gabriel did say, 'Fear not, Mary.' She was told that she would bear the Son of God, when the power of the Highest should overshadow her.

The Annunciation is followed for three verses, and the Nativity story for only one more. Then, at last, come the people, who simply do not fit. They can't be told

Like sister and brother, let's love one another

because they aren't sister and brother. At last, it was a Wassail. And we could recognize the voices in it. We should not expect a priest to sing a Wassail.

So those words [verses 26-35], transferred from Gospel to carol, were still following 'the Highest', and that was performed rightly by the priest! Both of us are trying to see how the story can fit a love-song. But he is trying to get the Nativity in, and I'm trying to get the Nativity out.

152

The tune, after all, is not from a choir. It's from the Wassail part of Devonshire. And it will return, to inspire the uninspired, the maids and lads, the 'great and small', to make them want to sing and to dance.

We've got the Wassail chorus of four lines, and we have the 'Nowell, Nowell, Nowell', and only one line doesn't fit – the line that tells 'of the angel Gabriel'. We are to rejoice in something new, novel and to do with birth. It is something to do with life, with love, 'And in our hearts rejoice'.

Now, how do I know I'm right and he's wrong? First, because he has left in parts of the old Wassail song. They are parts which are not in the Bible. Mary didn't say, 'Sir, what are ye?', nor

'Therefore I pray, depart away
For I stand in doubt of thee.'

Those must have been said by the girl to an unknown lover. Incidentally, Gabriel didn't look up in the virgin's face; nor had he given the news when Mary says she marvels at the tidings. The annunciation isn't made till the next verse! So what did the earthly girl wonder at?

This priest's very conscientiousness means he'd had to make many changes in the verses. He isn't a good enough rhymester to hide them. What he ought to have done was make rhymes inside the first, third, fifth and seventh lines. Look at verse 1 – and doubt me – and then look at verse 4. The converter couldn't cope.

Now, let us try to remake verse 2. Our task is easier. We have not got the piety to make the current verse. We shall only follow the pagan carol, and so make the new sense fit! Verse 2 is:

Mary anon looked him upon,
And said 'Sir, what are ye?
I marvel much at these tidings
Which thou has brought to me,
Married, I am, unto an old man
As the lot fell unto me;
Therefore, I pray, depart away
For I stand in doubt of thee.'

Line one, if we are to adopt Jenny, is OK. So it goes:

Jenny anon, looked him upon,
And said 'Sir, what are ye?
I marvel much ...'

The 'much' rhymes with 'touch'. See how the priest has altered its sense: 'Which thou has brought to me' has become a blank line there. And 'Married, I am, unto an old man' wouldn't be right, because Jenny isn't. It would be 'A maid I am, unknown to man.'

The last three lines are not Christian lines; and they are properly rhymed. So keep them, and the whole verse becomes:

Jenny anon, looked him upon,
And said, 'Sir, what are ye?
I marvel much ... touch
..................ee   [rhymes with 'ye']
A maid I am, unknown to man,
As the lot fell unto me,
Therefore, I pray, depart away,
For I stand in doubt of thee.'

Whatever she marvelled much at is the same thing that makes her doubt him. There are only a few places he could have touched. 'My breast so lovingly.'

Now we can have something new, novel and, eventually, to do with birth. At last we can sing the Wassail chorus:

Then sing we all both great and small
'Nowell, Nowell, Nowell';
Let us rejoice to give our voice
To the news we love to tell.

It is the same four-line verse, telling us to repeat the 'rejoice' after every single solo.

The Lovers' Carol

(Restored)

A young man came with heart aflame
Into the West Country,
And there he met a maiden yet
As fresh and fair as he.
When this bachelor was come to her
He kissed her lovingly,
And looking down in her bosom
He said 'I do love thee.'

Chorus:
Then sing we all both great and small
Nowell, Nowell, Nowell,
Let us rejoice to give our voice
To the news that we love to tell.

The maid anon looked him upon,
And said 'Sir, what do ye?
I marvel much that thou dost touch
My breast so lovingly.
A maid I am, unknown to man,
So life has been to me,
Therefore, I pray, depart away
For I stand in fear of thee.'
Chorus:

He said, 'Dear maid, be not afraid
But trust thyself to me,
The power of love, down from above,
Does now inspire me.
Thou can'st give relief, without a grief,
As love tells unto me,
And we can meet and fully greet
Each other nakedly.'
Chorus:

This came to pass, as his will was,
E'en as the young man told,
About midnight, that very night,
His arms did her enfold,
And they learned then, how, where and when
They might love long and well,
So all night long this was their song
'Nowell! Nowell! Nowell!'
Chorus:

Good people all, both great and small,
The which do hear my voice,
With one accord let's praise the word
That makes our hearts rejoice.
Like those two lovers let's love one another
While we our lives do spend,
And while we may, love happily,
So let my carol end.

Chorus:
Then sing we all, both great and small,
Nowell, Nowell, Nowell,
Let us rejoice to give our voice
To the news that we love to tell.

Spring Carols

The Holy Well
No. 56, OBC

As it fell out one May morning,
And upon a bright holiday,
Sweet Jesus asked of his dear mother
If he might go to play.
'To play, to play, sweet Jesus shall go,
And to play now get you gone;
And let me hear of no complaint
At night when you come home.'

Sweet Jesus went down to yonder town,
As far as the Holy Well,
And there did see as fine children
As any tongue can tell.
He said 'God bless you every one,
And your bodies Christ save and see!
And now, little children, I'll play with you,
And you shall play with me.'

But they made answer to him 'No!
Thou art meaner than us all;
Thou art but a simple fair maid's child,
Born in an ox's stall.'
Sweet Jesus turned him round about,
Neither laughed, nor smiled, nor spoke;
But the tears came trickling from his eyes
Like waters from the rock.

Sweet Jesus turned him round about,
To his mother's dear home went he,
And said, 'I have been in yonder town,
As after you may see;
I have been down in yonder town,
As far as the Holy Well;
There did I meet with as fine children
As any tongue can tell.

'I said, "God bless you every one,
And your bodies Christ save and see!
And now, little children, I'll play with you,
And you shall play with me."
But they made answer to me, "No",
They were lords' and ladies' sons,
And I the meanest of them all,
Born in an ox's stall.'

'Though you are but a maiden's child,
Born in an ox's stall,
Thou art the Christ, the King of Heaven,
And the Saviour of them all!
Sweet Jesus, go down to yonder town,
As far as the Holy Well,
And take away those sinful souls,
And dip them deep in hell.'

'Nay, nay' sweet Jesus smiled and said;
'Nay, nay, that may not be,
For there are too many sinful souls
Crying out for the help of me.'
Then up spoke the angel Gabriel,
Upon a good set *steven*,   [voice]
'Although you are but a maiden's child,
You are the King of heaven!'

Which is it to be, 'The Holy Well' or 'The Wishing Well'? I
choose 'The Wishing Well' because I think the song is a
folk-song, with a few plaster statuettes thrown in!

First, 'One May morning'. That's a give-away phrase.
Once a song is set on a bright holiday in May, it's almost
certainly a love-song. There are many folk-songs which begin
'As I roved out one May morning'. There is no Bible story
about Jesus that does so.

Following that opening, we have the lad going to the well
and being scorned by richer children; and the reactions of the
two plaster parent-figures. But May is courtship month, so
these children may be older than the Church carol allows.
Girls, scorning a lad, are more hurtful to him than other lads.

That would account for someone's wanting to 'dip them deep in hell'. Does that sound like the Virgin Mary or the lad's married mother?

And the other figure, who speaks up with a good, set voice, affirming the power of the lad – is that not like the father? The angel Gabriel was last heard declaring the birth of Jesus to Mary. We are asked to accept his reappearance. That is unlikely. His speech adds to the improbability. This Gabriel says that the lad, though but a maiden's child, is 'The King of Heaven'. But that does not answer the lad's own smiling statement:

> 'There are too many sinful souls
> Crying out for help of me.'

The good, set 'steven' should come out with something better, and more settling, than a repetition of the mother's reply.

Now to the third statuette, the lad himself. If he were Jesus, would he say, 'And your bodies Christ save and see'? He cannot refer to himself so impersonally. Nor should he be so careless as to say 'bodies' when he means souls!

The story itself has become confused in the careless conversion of the folk-song. This carol has two, almost identical, endings. One, when the mother says, 'Thou art the Saviour of them all'; the other when Gabriel says, 'You are the King of Heaven.' Obviously the claim, in whatever form of words, must come once only, at the end of the song. Its nature can be seen through the associations of the word 'Saviour'. Lads and men spend their lives trying to save women. So, 'You are the saviour of them all' – in some masculine sense – was the original meaning of the ending. That does follow the lad's smiling statement 'For there are too many ... Crying out for help of me'. It is a good, set answer, given by an older man, to the first rejection his son has received from girls, to say, 'You can save the lot of them!'

The Wishing Well

(Restored)

Solo, Man:
As it fell out one May morning
On a bright holiday,
Young Tom did ask of his fond mother
If he might go to play

Chorus:
If he might go to play.

'To play, to play, then you shall go,
To play now get you gone,
But let me hear of no complaint
At night when you come home.'

Chorus:
At night when you come home.

Young Tom went down to yonder town
As far as the Wishing Well,
And there he saw pretty maidens, fair
As any tongue can tell.

Chorus:
As any tongue can tell.

He said 'Good-morrow, everyone,
Your beauty's fair to see;
And now sweet maids I'll play with you,
And you shall play with me.'

Chorus:
And you shall play with me.

But they made answer to him 'No,
You're poorer than us all,
You are a simple labourer's son,
Born in a cottage small.'

Chorus:
Born in a cottage small.

Young Tom he turned him round about,
He neither smiled nor spoke,
But tears came trickling down from his eyes
Like water from a rock.

Chorus:
Like water from a rock.

Young Tom he turned him round about
And to his home went he,
And there he told to his fond mother
What he did speak and see.
Chorus: What he did speak and see.

His mother cried in angry tone
'Go down to yonder well,
And drive away all those scornful girls,
And bid them all farewell.'
Chorus: And bid them all farewell.

'No, No,' young Tom he smiled and said,
'No, No, that may not be,
I like too much all those proud young girls
That stand so fair to see.'
Chorus: That stand so fair to see.

Then his father spoke with old wisdom,
In a loud and certain tone,
'A lad may be but a poor man's son,
He's the lord of all women!'
Chorus: He's the lord of all women!

Down in Yon Forest
No. 61, OBC

Down in yon forest there stands a hall:
It's covered all over with purple and pall:

Refrain:
The bells of paradise I heard them ring;
And I love my lord Jesus above anything.

In that hall there stands a bed:
It's covered all over with scarlet so red:
Refrain:

At the bed-side there lies a stone:
Which the sweet Virgin Mary knelt upon:
Refrain:

Under that bed there runs a flood:
The one half runs water, the other runs blood:
Refrain:

At the bed's foot there grows a thorn:
Which ever blows blossom since he was born:
Refrain:

Over that bed the moon shines bright:
Denoting our Saviour was born this night:
Refrain:

OTHER VERSIONS:
Can you dry it on yonder thorn,
Parsley, sage, rosemary and thyme,
Which never bore blossom since Adam was born?
And you shall be a true lover of mine.

From 'The Ballad of The Cambric Shirt'

There are only three Christian lines. The first, 'And I love my lord Jesus above everything', does not follow 'The bells of Paradise I heard them ring.' The second, 'Which the sweet Virgin Mary knelt upon', only follows 'At the bed-side there lies a stone' in so far as anyone can kneel on any stone. But what stone, by what bed, did the Virgin Mary ever kneel on? The third, 'Denoting our Saviour was born this night', cannot be 'denoted' from 'Over that bed the moon shines bright.' Whoever 'denoted' that wanted to give an explanation that doesn't explain.

So take them out and make sense of what's left! The 'forest', for woman's sexual hair, is still used today. The 'hall', inside the forest, is a natural symbol. The 'White Bird Featherless', in the restored nursery rhyme of that name, flew wingless into the great inner hall. That does lead to paradise! For paradise is not Christian heaven. It's happiness. The happiest experience known to the folk is sexual love.

The bed, in 'scarlet so red', inside the hall, is velvet flesh. The 'stone' I took to be an egg-stone. The flood is the flood of passion. The 'thorn' is confirmed as a man's sexual symbol – like 'prickle' – by the verse from the 'The Ballad of the Cambric Shirt', quoted in the 'Other Versions'. That 'thorn', in one sense, never bears blossom since Adam was born – as the ballad says. In another sense, it ever does, as the carol says!

When the thorn is growing at the bed's foot, and the moon is shining bright, what does it denote? Someone is going to be conceived that night!

That's my explanation. Compare it with this, from the footnotes to the carol in the OBC – 'The mystical meaning … was therefore eucharistic, the altar and the sacrifice, while the thorn and other allusions point to an interweaving of the legend of the Holy Grail.' You'll enjoy that.

Down in Yon Forest

(Restored)

Solo, man:
Down in yon forest there stands a hall,
Hung all about with purple and pall.

The bells of the steeple I hear them ring,
I love sweet Jenny above anything.

Within that hallway there stands a bed,
Bedecked all over with scarlet and red.
Refrain:

At that bed-head there stops a stone,
Set all in snow-white, and all alone.
Refrain:

Beneath that bed-side there starts a flood,
Flowing all jet-black as a deep river's blood,
Refrain:

Before that bed-foot there stems a thorn,
Thrusting all rose-bloom since Adam was born.
Refrain:

Upon that bed-post the moon strikes bright,
Bringing all honey-moon this very night!

Refrain:
The bells of the steeple I hear them ring,
I love sweet Jenny above anything.

My Dancing Day
No. 71, OBC

Tomorrow shall be my dancing day:
I would my true love did so chance
To see the legend of my play,
To call my true love to my dance:

Refrain:
Sing O my love, O my love, my love, my love:
This have I done for my true love.

Then was I born of a virgin pure,
Of her I took fleshly substance:
Thus was I knit to man's nature
To call my true love to my dance:

Refrain:
In a manger laid and wrapped I was,
So very poor, this was my chance,
Betwixt an ox and a silly poor ass,
To call my true love to my dance.

Refrain:
Then afterwards baptized I was;
The Holy Ghost on me did glance,
My Father's voice heard from above,
To call my true love to my dance:

Refrain:
Into the desert I was led,
Where I fasted without substance;
The devil bade me make stones my bread,
To have me break my true love's dance:

Refrain:
The Jews on me they made great suit,
And with me made great variance,

166

Because they loved darkness rather than light,
To call my true love to my dance:

Refrain:
For thirty pence Judas me sold
His covetousness for to advance;
'Mark whom I kiss, the same do hold,'
The same is he shall lead the dance:

Refrain:

OTHER VERSIONS:
This carol goes on for four more verses. As I do not use them
in my restoration, for reasons I give in my explanation, I
quote them here.

Before Pilate the Jews me brought,
Where Barabbas had deliverance;
They scourged me and set me at nought,
Judged me to die to lead the dance.

Then on the cross hanged I was,
Where a spear to my heart did glance;
There issued forth both water and blood,
To call my true love to my dance.

Then down to hell I took my way
For my true love's deliverance
And rose again on the third day,
Up to my true love and the dance.

Then up to heaven I did ascend,
Where now I dwell in sure substance
On the right hand of God, that man
May come unto the general dance.

[The refrain is between each of the above verses.]

The refrain should be printed beneath each verse of the
Christianized carol so that the contrast between it and the
verse shall be repeatedly shown. One or the other is wrong. If

there should be a rhymed-up version of Christ's life, the refrain is too loving. If there should be a love-song, the verses are too Christian.

Which is the original? I think the refrain is, because that very first verse is still a love-song's. 'Tomorrow shall be my dancing day' means, to me, 'Tomorrow shall be my wedding day.' The alternative explanation is 'Tomorrow I shall be in heaven.' But that won't do, because 'Tomorrow' after verse seven, is the day of the Crucifixion. After verse eleven there is no tomorrow! Heaven as a dance-hall is a very rare image in Christian mythology.

The interpretation of 'dancing day' must go with one's interpretation of 'my true love'. By mental contortion, that can be forced to mean something other than 'my true love'. It can be made to mean God, as in 'And rose again on the third day/Up to my true love and the dance' (verse 10). But to call God to Jesus's dance is too far a call for me. Or Jesus's true love might be said to be man. But then there would be verse 7, 'Mark whom I kiss, the same do hold/The same is he shall lead the dance.' Judas?! These strained meanings are signs of alteration.

The natural sense of that first verse and first refrain cannot be denied. 'This is probably based on a secular song,' says the editor of the *Oxford Book of Carols*. If it were not, we'd have no verse 1! For the legend of Christ's life begins in verse 2 and does not follow that beginning. Now, it's far more likely, and far more common, to begin in the old way and then change, than to begin in a new way and then revert. It's the conclusion that concludes. Look at that length of teaching – eleven verses of it.

We have the love-song's beginning. The rest is the love-song altered. But not completely altered, or we wouldn't have the jumble we do have. If the re-writer takes a completely freehand, as Neale did in 'Good King Wenceslas' and Nahum Tate in 'While Shepherds Watched', he can construct a consistent hymn. It's when he retains some of the old with the new that all kinds of inconsistencies – in form, as well as matter – can be detected. We will detect the remnants of the old love-song.

The first verse tells us what to look for in the others –

I would my true love did so chance
To hear the legend of my play

– the story of my life. The Christian took that meaning and
changed it to the story of Jesus's life. We must look for the
history of a young man or woman.

Verse 7 tells us clearly which of the two it is –

Mark whom I kiss, the same do hold,
The same is he shall lead the dance ...

It does say 'he'. So 'I' is a woman – and, as we are looking for
traces of a love-song, those inverted commas should be
extended, and she might sing, today, 'See the man I kiss and
hold. He's the one who'll lead my dance.' I judge, also, that
the intense feeling of the refrain is more fitting, in a traditional
folk-song, to a woman than a man; as is the feeling of the
importance of the wedding day.

We are, then, going to look for the story of a young
woman's life in, and under, the Bible narrative.

In verse 2 it is logical to replace

I was born of a virgin pure,
Of her I took fleshly substance

with 'I was born a woman sure,/My mother gave me her
substance', because that heredity leads properly in to 'Thus
was I knit to man's nature.' Being born of a virgin pure does
not knit her to human nature.

In verse 3 the link between the girl's early life and the
adaptation into Christ's is the 'very poor'. She's a girl of the
people, a typical heroine of the folk.

Verse 4 is later, after something or other on her did glance.
The word 'glance' does not fit the Holy Ghost, so it must be a
retained rhyme-word. After that, she hears some voice call
her true love to her dance. The carol has 'my Father's', but I
think we can reasonably restore that to 'Nature's'.

Verse 5 has the end-line changed. It becomes 'To have
me break my true love's dance'. The devil has bidden her

169

make stones her bread. Some temptation or other has tried to mislead her. The temptation that would lead a poor girl from her love, and that has to do with bread, is the temptation of riches. The devil is some man who is trying to buy her.

Verse 6 is another trial. Someone, something, is upsetting her a great deal. I thought the word 'suit' (again liable to be a retained rhyme word) gave a clue, for, although law-suit might be used to describe the Jew's accusation, I thought it more likely to be a love-suit. That would follow the previous verse's account of someone trying to seduce her with money. 'And with me made great variance' applies better to upsetting a girl with an unwanted love-suit than charging Christ with blasphemy.

Verse 7 was the conclusion of the love-song because of those last two lines,

'Mark whom I kiss, the same do hold,'
The same is he shall lead the dance.

It sounds like the end; and, for the first time, the singer uses the future tense, looks forward to the coming marriage. The first two lines of the verse have the clue 'advance' in them (who ever heard of covetousness advancing?). They must refer to her lover and so lead in to the 'Mark whom I kiss.'

Confirmation of the hypothesis that the song did end at verse 7 will be found by examining the additional verses. If they are carelessly made, they are likely to be the work of a moralizer.

Verses 9 and 11 show the carelessness. 'Was' does not rhyme with 'blood'. 'Ascend' does not rhyme with 'man'.

Where the verses do rhyme, they do so by using words which have been used before. 'Glance', in verse 9 has been used twice before in the first seven verses. 'Substance', in verse 11 has been used once. There is only one new rhyme with 'dance' in all the four verses – 'deliverance'. And that is used twice. The Franciscan friar Ryman who wrote this version has been careless as well as uninspired. Read pages 131-2 of *Who Really Killed Cock Robin?*!

My Dancing Day
(Restored)

Solo, Woman:
Today shall be my dancing day,
I would the whole world did so chance
To hear the story of my way
To call my true love to my dance.

Refrain:
Sing O my love, O my love, my love, my love,
This have I done for my true love.

Oh I was born a woman, sure,
My mother gave me her substance,
Thus was I knit to our nature
To call my true love to my dance.
Refrain:

In cradle laid and wrapped I was,
So very poor, so was my chance,
'Twixt straw and wool, a simple lass,
To call my true love to my dance.
Refrain:

When I was grown, a young maiden,
The power of love on me did glance,
My nature's voice heard from within,
To call my true love to my dance.
Refrain:

Into the city I was led,
Where I did gather no sustenance,
I dreamed of him, and begged my bread,
To call my true love to my dance.
Refrain:

Merchants for me they made long suit,
And with me made great variance,
But I'd not sell my body's fruit,
To call my true love to my dance.
Refrain:

All for my love I did refuse,
His honour proudly to advance,
See him I kiss? Now do I choose
To call my true love to my dance.

Refrain:
Sing O my love, O my love, my love, my love,
This have I done for my true love.

The Cherry Tree Carol
No. 66, OBC

Joseph was an old man,
And an old man was he,
When he wedded Mary
In the land of Galilee.

Joseph and Mary
Walked through an orchard good,
Where was cherries and berries
So red as any blood.

Joseph and Mary
Walked through an orchard green,
Where was berries and cherries
As thick as might be seen.

O then bespoke Mary,
With words so meek and mild,
'Pluck me one cherry, Joseph,
For I am with child.'

O then bespoke Joseph
With answer most unkind,
'Let him pluck thee a cherry
That brought thee now with child.'

O then bespoke the baby
Within his mother's womb –
'Bow down then the tallest tree
For my mother to have some.'

Then bowed down the highest tree,
Unto his mother's hand.
Then she cried 'See, Joseph,
I have cherries at command.'

O then bespoke Joseph
'I have done Mary wrong;
But now, cheer up, my dearest,
And do not be cast down.

'O eat your cherries, Mary,
O eat your cherries now,
O eat your cherries, Mary,
That grow upon the bough.'

Then Mary plucked a cherry
As red as any blood;
Then Mary she went homewards
All with her heavy load.

'This was one of the most popular Carols' is part of the footnote in the OBC. This was. And it is not now. It's the alteration of the story that's done it – for the tune is as good as ever.

What we have to do is fight off Joseph and Mary, for a further young man and a further young woman. We must dispose of Joseph, of whom it says,

Joseph was an old man,
And an old man was he.

Then we can dispose of Mary, and of her son, Jesus, who can work miracles.

In their place, we can substitute a man who is ignorant. He can be made to understand that the tallest tree bows down to a girl's hand. Then she will go homeward with her heavy load.

The reasons are these. Joseph and Mary cannot walk through an 'orchard green'; and for ever more, not through a symbolic 'orchard red'. Joseph cannot make use of his old phallus – not according to the Bible story. But to a young fellow and a young girl, this act is undoubtedly significant. He will see her walk, in fulfilment, to many a fertile marriage.

For this is an English orchard. How right it is for an English couple! How wrong it would be for a biblical, old married couple!

174

It is Joseph who speaks to her. He says, impossible to argue with him,

'Let him pluck thee a cherry
That brought thee now with child.'

He believes her to be pregnant. And to him the unborn child answers:

'Bow down then the tallest tree
For my mother to have some.'

But a cherry tree is not a God symbol. It is universally respected as a man's symbol. There is a way of calling 'Cherry ripe' to every girl, since Herrick first sang it. There is:

I gave my love a cherry
Without any stone,
I gave my love a chicken
Without any bone.

That's an American folk-song about real people, about making children. For, with any purpose, English or American, real things do bend down to a girl's hand.

I saw that someone reading his apocryphal Bible, came across this: 'Whereupon the little child Jesus, sitting with a glad countenance in his mother's lap, saith to the palm "O tree, bend down the branches."' He describes that as a variant of Joseph and Mary. But here it is not a variant. The child had been born in Bethlehem and was now taken to the desert, and there he made the palm tree bow down with its branches. Here, it is an unborn child. He never had a 'glad countenance' that could make the cherry tree, with the most powerful branches, bow down. In every case, it was a miracle. But with Robin – 'a simple lad was he' – and Jenny I made everything happen naturally again. And it was not a miracle, to speak miraculously!

Finally, I want to remember D.H. Lawrence: 'At the Brewsters' home beside the lake of Kandy, Lawrence and Frieda often sang as they sat on the verandah in the after-glow of sunset. Achsah Brewster remembers their singing "The Cherry Tree Carol', a Carol which greatly pleased Lawrence, expecially the last verse in which the father of the baby (God) bends down the branch of the cherry tree for the Virgin Mary to pluck a fruit, thus proving her innocence, and allaying Joseph's fears. This seemed to have a special significance for Lawrence.'

Achsah Brewster, quoted on p. 41 of a booklet by the
D.H. Lawrence Society, Blaketon Hall, Eastwood,
Nottingham.

The Cherry Tree Carol
(Restored. Tune – the second tune in the OBC)

Now Robin was a young lad,
A simple lad was he,
He went and married Jenny
In the English country.

Young Robin and his Jenny
Walked through an orchard green,
Where cherries were and berries were
As thick as might be seen.

O then upspoke his Jenny
With words so meek and mild,
'O give to me a cherry,
I want one for my child.'

O then replied young Robin
With answer rude and wild,
'Go pluck yourself your own cherry
If it is for your child.'

O now was heard the baby,
That yet was not begun,
'Bow down the tallest cherry
My mother must have one.'

Then bowèd down the tallest
Into his mother's hand;
Then Jenny said 'See, Robin, see,
I've cherries at command.'

Then simply answered Robin
'I did not understand.
I'll give the tallest cherry
That grows in England.'

Young Robin and his Jenny
Walked through an orchard red
Where cherries were and berries were
As thick as might be spread.

O eat your cherries, Jenny,
O eat your cherries now,
O eat your cherries cheerfully
That ripen on the bough.

Then Jenny plucked the cherries
As red as any blood;
And after went contented home
With all her fruitful load.

The Miraculous Harvest
No. 55, OBC

Rise up, rise up, you merry men all,
See that you ready be:
All children under two years old
Now slain they all shall be.

Then Jesus, aye, and Joseph,
And Mary that was unknown,
They travelled by a husbandman,
Just while his seed was sown.

'God speed your work' said Jesus,
'Throw all your seed away,
And carry home as ripened corn
What you have sown this day;

'For to keep your wife and family
From sorrow, grief, and pain,
And keep Christ in remembrance
Till seed-time comes again.'

The husbandman fell on his knees,
Even upon his face;
'Long time hast thou been looked for,
But now thou'rt come at last.

'And I myself do now believe
Thy name is Jesus called,
Redeemer of mankind thou art,
Though undeserving all.'

After that there came King Herod,
With his train so furiously,
Enquiring of the husbandman
Whether Jesus had passed by.

'Why, the truth it must be spoke,
And the truth it must be known,
For Jesus he passed by this way,
Just as my seed was sown.

'But now I have it reapen,
And some laid in my wain,
Ready to fetch and carry
Into my barn again.'

'Turn back,' then says the Captain.
'Your labour and mine's in vain:
It's full three-quarters of a year
Since he his seed has sown.'

So Herod was deceived
By the work of God's own hand:
No further he proceeded
Into the Holy Land.

There's thousands of children young,
Which for his sake did die;
Do not forbid those little ones,
And do not them deny.

If only I can point out the mistakes … if I can show you an error which will reveal the first verse. Let me quote it again:

Rise up, rise up, you merry men all,
See that you ready be;
All children under two years old
Now slain they all shall be.

The first is a call to 'Rise up'. The second is a call that all children under two years old shall be slain. Are you paying attention?

Once, and today, Cock Robin makes all men merry. And Robin Hood has merry men. There, we're being summoned, being made to get ready. That is why the horn, half-heard, is blowing. Can we make it heard even more clearly?

Why is Robin calling us after all these years? Because he wants us to sing a song so old that it goes back to when people fucked in the meadows to make the corn come up. Remember that, next time you're summoned to rise up, you are summoned to rouse the earth. It is the waking of both.

Maid Marian is still asleep. How can any woman be merry with those two lines:

All children under two years old
Now slain they all shall be?

Only if the lines are corrected. Every woman must continue instead to the very end. There, she will find:

Do not forbid those little ones,
And do not them deny.

Now, if she puts them together, she'll have:

Rise up, rise up, you merry men all,
See that you ready be,

which can join with the other!

It's mad fertility. This carol, the nursery rhymes, folk-songs, the Museums of Man, people's talk: they're all going to ripen to come to the Harvest Festival. It will not only be one Harvest Festival but the two, living together. By the power of Robin Redbreast, or Robin Hood.

The preaching friars got the apocryphal legends into the carol. Of course, there is no such official explanation. But apparently there is an unofficial explanation, described in the Acts of Thomas 10 (whoever he was). That is an unmerry lie that says: 'The notion of a harvest springing straight out a new-sown seed may be compared to [I like this comparison] where Jesus scatters a handful of seed which at once produces a hundred measures of wheat.' This is according to the Reverend Erik Routley in *The English Carol*. He was too late for the preaching friars.

But here it was not Jesus who scattered; it was the husbandman. Jesus produces a harvest quickly. And the husbandman deceives King Herod. By the same trick he tries to make him forget the mating. For three-quarters of a year are nine months! It takes the same time for a crop of corn to be ripe as for a baby to be born – 'A Miraculous Harvest' from a physical, bodily, likeness. That is why we call sperm 'seed'. We have absorbed the term without noticing that it is done. And it's sown in a furrow, a furrow in Mother Earth, once more noticeable to the human eye.

By a husbandman! We get double meaning not by being literary but by perceiving that two things are alike, mother and earth, husband and husbandman. When a husband sows his seed in his wife, that very moment the seed is ripened. Oh, what a mystic word! And indeed it is mystic. Laid in his wife's womb, just at the moment that cannot be halted, it can be carried into the barn or into the home and shall be born when harvest-time comes.

The God-like figure, who presides over the fertility of wife and of harvest is Robin Redbreast. He has two companions, Dobbin and John. These three are much older than the Three Wise Men. They occur in 'Hunting The Wren'. It is they who can overcome the denial of the winter.

So the original carol did not say,

So Herod was deceived
By the work of God's own hand;
No further he proceeded
Into the Holy Land.

(Look at the word 'proceeded' in that verse.) The verse did not confirm that Herod couldn't go further into the Holy Land.

The original carol, also, did not say,

'Turn back,' then says the Captain,
'Your labour and mine's in vain;
It's full three-quarters of a year
Since he his seed has sown.'

Three quarters of a year did not make Jesus escape Herod. But Robin, and his two wise men, given nine months can

make life flow for ever in England or in the Holy Land.
Because of that, we can live for ever.

The Miraculous Harvest

(Restored)

Chorus:
Rise up, rise up, you merry men all,
See that you ready, ready, be,
All children unto you they call
And born they all must be.

Solo:
Robin, Robin and Dobbin too,
And John were all unknown,
They travelled to a husbandman
Whose seed was not yet sown.
'Good luck! Good luck!' said Red Robin,
'Sow all your seed away,
'And carry home as ripened corn
What you will sow this day.'
Chorus:

Husband, husband, fell on his knee
And then upon his face,
'Long time have I been waiting thee
To sow my seed in place.'
And I, and I, do now perceive
Why thou art Robin called,
The maker of mankind art thou
With thy red blood so bold.'
Chorus:

And then, and then, came Winter old
Who would all life destroy,
And he did ask the husbandman
If Robin passed that way.
'Indeed, indeed, he has been here,
The truth it must be known,

For Robin's three did pass by me
Just as my seed was sown.'
Chorus:

'And now, and now, it's ripened
And it is laid in wain,*
And it has just been carried
Into my home again.'
'Away, away,' said Winter old,
'My frost and snow is vain,
'Tis full three-quarters of a year
Since he has sown this grain.'
Chorus:

Winter, winter, he was deceived
By the work of Robin's band,
No further could he conquer
In this our English land.
Thousands, thousands, of children small
Wait for us night and day,
Do not deny those little ones,
And do not them delay!

Chorus:
Rise up, rise up, you merry men all
See that you ready, ready, be,
All children unto you they call
And born they all must be.

* 'Wame' means womb. Winter hears 'wain' (waggon), as the husbandman
meant he should.

Dutch Carol
No. 73, OBC

A child is born in Bethlehem;
Awaiteth him all Jerusalem.

Chorus:
Amor, amor, amor, amor, amor,
Quam dulcis est amor!

The Son took upon him humanity,
That to the Father thus draws nigh.
Chorus:

The angels above were singing then,
Below were rejoicing the shepherd men.
Chorus:

Now let us all with the angels sing,
Yea, now let our hearts for gladness spring.
Chorus:

Why go into Dutch carols? Because the chorus caught my
eye: 'Love, love, love, love, love'. Then, next line – just to
confirm it's not Christian love, or platonic love, or spiritual,
or mystical, or transcendental or ineffable love – comes 'How
sweet it is to love.'
  All around that are verses of rubbish. Wouldn't you go to a
Dutchman calling out 'Help!' if he were drowning?
Drowning? Yes, look at the other lines in the other verses.
  We've got to pick such clues out of it. Whoever pushed him
in is very careless. Fancy turning the chorus into Latin and
thinking that would disguise it enough! So don't let's be too
clever. Let's just turn the Christian flotsam back into a
love-song.
  'Someone, a man or a girl, is born; awaits him or her all the
town. The boy-girl takes on human nature; and that draws

the other to him/her. Women sing above [this is probably what the traditional verse does]. Men sing below [that is the happy sex-meeting]. Then let's all be happy and make love.'

That is it. The chorus says 'Make love.' And, while in passing, let us note that in Chaucer the nun who wore a motto '*Amor vincit omnia*'. ('Love conquers everything', for those people who didn't speak Latin) would have drawn many men near in Holland. Love is very good at seeing the hidden meaning in people, and even in carols.

The King and Queen Carol
(Restored)

A girl is born in a world of men
They wait on her every one of them!

Chorus:
With love, with love, with love, with love,
How sweet it is to love with love!

The girl is queen by her nature,
But one man shall be over her!
Chorus:

The man on high is singing now,
The girl is singing down below!
Chorus:

And soon majestically we'll sing
When woman's queen and man is king!

Chorus:
With love, with love, with love, with love,
How sweet it is to love with love!

Adam Lay Ybounden
No. 180, OBC

Adam lay ybounden,
Bounden in a bond:
Four thousand winter
Thought he not too long.

And all was for an apple,
And apple that he took,
As clerkes finden written
In their book.

Ne had the apple taken been
The apple taken been,
Ne had never our lady
A-been heavene queen.

Blessed be the time
That apple taken was,
Therefore we moun singen
Deo gracias.

The crux is in verse 3:

Ne hadde the apple taken been,
The apple taken been,
Ne had never our lady
A-been heavene queen.

Swallow that, and you swallow the worm in the apple!

Who put it there? Who is 'heavene queen'? And who also wrote, incidentally, the '*Deo gracias*' in verse four. Who wanted it put there?

Now, how do I prove that it is a worm? First, by the meaning of those four lines themselves. Adam's biting of the apple is not mourned as a sin but turned into a rejoicing that it

made Mary, mother of the second Adam, heaven's queen. By that logic, Adam's fall is not only necessary but a good thing. Now, you can – if you wish – call that a Christian paradox. But before you take that easy escape, consider this:

Four thousand winter
Thought he not too long.

That is verse 1. Adam did not find his 'bond' much of a punishment! It doesn't sound like being driven out of the Garden of Eden with a flaming sword. Nor does it sound like the ills of mankind from then to the coming of Christ, and to the present day. It sounds as if he enjoyed it.
Then consider this:

And all was for an apple,
An apple that he took.

It's a small thing. And yet it's a big thing. A poet can write something human about it. But a celibate monk does consider it as a vast one. He thinks that neither man or woman should do it! Mankind's progress must not go on. That is why I say that the worm is not part of the apple.

The song, if genuine, would have had to be composed by a cleric in holy orders. Yet the song speaks of them as priests apart:

> As clerkes finden written
> In their book.

That is the voice of the original poet, who did not consider himself one of them, or his book, their book! He cannot go onto the final verse:

> Therefore we moun singen
> *Deo gracias.*

He cannot use 'therefore'; and he never uses Latin! What we have to do is return to verse 3 and ask, 'What would have happened to our girl if the apple had not been taken?'

Once the Old Adam is re-awakened, he soon speaks modern English! What happened was that the rewriting stopped the song being sung, and therefore prevented its language being continually modernized. So we find the archaic English in which it was written, preserved. For this song is not as old as the Wassails or the-holly-and-the-ivy songs or 'I Saw Three Ships'. This is a personal lyric, and here it uses folk-imagery to be personal. Here, everything – from the bond, the 4,000 winters' decisions and the apple – is folk imagery, but also individual.

So here is restored not a pagan song, going back to pre-Christian times, but a secular, sexual, happy song that is pagan only because its attitude is scientific, commonly called pagan. The taking of an apple is sexual, for both of them, for Adam and for Eve, for all of us.

Adam's Bound

(Restored)

Adam lay a-bounden,
A-bounden in a bond,
Forty thousand winters
Found he not too long.

And all was for an apple,
An apple that he took,
As the clerks find written
In their bounden book.

Had it not been taken,
Oh, taken in a bound!
Not another woman
Had on earth been found!

Boundless is the bonding
Now that apple taken is,
Men are bound to sing-en,
Sing their joy for this!

Jacob's Ladder
No. 58, OBC

As Jacob with travel was weary one day,*
At night on a stone for a pillow he lay;
He saw in a vision a ladder so high
That its foot was on earth and its top in the sky.

Chorus:
Alleluia to Jesus, who died on the tree
And hath raised up a ladder of mercy for me,
And hath raised up a ladder of mercy for me.

This ladder is long, it is strong and well-made,
Has stood hundreds of years and is not yet decayed;
Many millions have climbed it and reached Sion's hill,
And thousands by faith are climbing it still.
Chorus:

Come, let us ascend! all may climb it who will;
For the angels of Jacob are guarding it still;
And remember, each step that by faith we pass o'er,
Some martyr or prophet hath trod it before:
Chorus:

And when we arrive at the haven of rest,
We shall hear the glad words 'Come up hither, ye blest,
Here are regions of light, here are mansions of bliss.'
Oh, who would not climb such a ladder as this?
Chorus:

'This is apparently a carol to which new words were fitted under the influence of the Methodist Revival.' Eh? Who wrote that? The editor of the *Oxford Book of Carols*. He

* 'And he took the stones of that place, and put them for his pillows': Genesis, 28, verse 11.

makes the apparent disappear before your very eyes! What if he'd written, 'This is obviously a popular song to which Christian words were fitted-up under the influence of the Methodist connival'?

Why did he have to write it at all? Because the discrepancies between this song and the Bible story are so great. Of course, it wasn't Jesus who raised up a ladder of mercy. Jesus wasn't even born. Come to that, it wasn't even Jacob! Jacob dreamed he saw it. The ladder – should you wish to believe in the Old Testament – is not still standing. All may not climb it who will. Angels, only, were ascending and descending. Jehovah stood at the top, declaring ... Zionist propaganda (Genesis 28, verses 10-19).

Folk don't like climbing an 'old' ladder of mercy, whatever that means. They like climbing present ladders. Ladders that are strong and well-made that have stood hundreds of years and are not yet decayed, that lead to folk-heaven, now. That's why the tense changes. The Ladder *is*, not only was. And, I think, it was the ladder of Adam (though it can't be proved like this).

Isn't it miraculous (O, Miraculous Harvest) that the term 'Jacob's Ladder' is recorded in *Partridge's Dictionary of Historical Slang*? 'Jacob is the male member. Jacob's Ladder is in the leg of ballet girl's tights; the female pudend, from Jacob (first sense) and Ladder (last sense). It was in the nineteenth century, low.' Good old Partridge! He's in 'climb', and 'the pear tree' is in the distance! I've heard the folk use the phrase in song at our folk club:

And if he is a son, my dear,
Buy him the breeches blue,
And he will climb the rigging
Just like I'm climbing you!

Oh Methodists, wasn't there madness in stealing that ladder? For now you have a record of theft. And someone will use that, to find you're guilty of other thefts, where the evidence is not so strong. You pinched it, and now you are saying it comes from Jesus!

Christians, Jews and other folk of the world, do you know what Jacob did after the dream? Because Jehovah had promised him that his seed should be as numerous as the dust of the earth, 'He took the stone that he had put for his pillows, and set it for a pillar, and poured oil on top of it.' So the ladder isn't only an English likeness. It's Jewish; and extends to the Hindus. They pour oil over a pillar-stone and call it the lingam. I wonder how many other people have the ladder as a long, strong, well-made erection? Did Adam? 'Oh man, what art thou when thy cock is up?' – Nathaniel Fields in *Amends for Ladies*, 1618. For men, the phallus creates the human race. For Christian men, Adam does!

The Ladder

(Restored)

As Adam was weary with working one day,
At noon on two stones for his pillows he lay,
When he saw in a vision a ladder so high
Its foot was on earth but its top in the sky!

Chorus:
Yoop-ai-adee for Adam who dreamed manfully
And has raised up a ladder of comfort for me.

This ladder is long, it is strong and well-made,
Has stood hundreds of years and is not yet decayed.
Many millions have climbed it and reached to the moon,
And someone here present will be climbing it soon!
Chorus:

Oh still it will stand, we may climb if we will,
For the strength of Old Adam is raising it still,
And remember each time that we climb to the top,
No man and no woman has ever said 'Stop!'
Chorus:

And when we arrive at our home in the sky,
We shall hear the glad whisper 'Come, rise it on high!

Here are regions of rapture, here are mansions of bliss!'
Oh, who would not climb such a ladder as this?

Chorus:
Yoop-ai-adee for Adam who dreamed manfully
And has raised up a ladder of comfort for me.

The Pelican

No. 13, *English Folk Song Journal*

As I was a-walking down by a wilderness,
There was I assaulted by many wild beasts,
And there I did hear a bird making her moan
That the young ones had fled and gone far from their
   home.

Then she followed me down to the yonder green grove,
And searched for those young ones that had all gone from
   home,
And when she had found them, how so sad were they,
And cold was the harbour wherein they did lay.

Then she took them safe home all at her own breast,
And she fed them with some *dillon** and food of the best,
And she spared them some blood that came from her own
   breast,
And she bid them drink freely and leave home no more.

[* dill-water]

An old man in Southampton Workhouse sang that in 1906.
He lasted long enough to pass it on to a collector. But the
sense of the song has gone. Babble is beginning. The old
fighter has been battered into semi-consciousness by
Victorian values.

But the collector was perfectly conscious – he was like the referee counting ten. 'This song is an illustration of the popular superstition that the pelican feeds its young with blood from its own breast. See *Chambers' Encyclopaedia*, under pelican. In architecture, the pelican is an emblem of Christ or the Christian Church. The young ones that had fled and gone far from their home, but return at last to their mother, will therefore be those who have strayed from the Church and afterwards returned to it' (*English Folk-Song Journal*). He raises the parson's hand. A technical knock-out. The old singer is slumped in the corner.

He can't argue, as I do, against the flat announcement. He can't protest, as I do, against that 'therefore' – when there isn't any 'therefore'. He can't say 'Are heretics and sinners young ones?'

Let me get my blow in. It is ridiculous to picture the Church following anyone down to a grove. Especially a Church looking like a pelican. And 'green grove' too. That's a folk-scene for love. It's not where heretics go.

Who mentioned pelicans anyway? The bird isn't named in the song. Was it the collector, who worked out the title from his Christian assumptions and then printed it in block capitals at the head of the song? That would prejudice the meaning a bit, wouldn't it? Or did the old singer say, 'I'm going to sing you a song about a pelican?' (His beak can hold more than his belly can.) How popular was that superstition? Have you heard of it? It's not an English folk bird, like robin, wren, lark and cuckoo. I think it only nests in *Chambers' Encyclopaedia*.

It's true my own assumptions are that the English peasants did not sing songs about a flat-footed Church flopping after heretics and sinners down to green groves to save them from starvation. It's true I think the folk sang folk-songs. 'As I was a-walking' does sound like one. But, from these general prejudices, I move to particular reasons why this song is a love-song.

This bird is 'she'. Now birds being 'she' is indeed a modern superstition! She follows 'me' down to the grove. 'Me' is a man. He's been walking, alone, by a wilderness and is there attacked. Then he hears a woman 'making her moan' – it must be an old song.

All is clear so far. And, if only she had lost her children, the story would be straightforward. But that doesn't explain what happens next. Why should she be so lucky as to find the young ones in that very grove man led her to? And no woman – only a pelican in books – can feed the youngsters with blood.

Let's recap. The man's walking, somewhere way out in the country. There he's attacked by unnamed wild beasts. With what injuries we're not told. And, by sheer coincidence again – there and then he hears the woman complaining. Any woman? Some woman unknown to him? Hardly; she must know him well or she wouldn't follow him down into any wood. That she does follow him shows the couple are, or have been, lovers.

Now, what is the trouble? Has she lost her kids or has she lost him? I think the second. And so she has not lost The Young Ones, plural, but The Young One, singular. That's why she can search and find this Young One in the privacy of the spring wood. That's why the man can disappear from the song. His place is taken by his male symbol.

And when she finds him, what? He's cold and lying down. The man doesn't want her.

What can she do? Rouse him, show him her breasts. And what comes out of her breasts? Not blood: milk! She's pregnant – very pregnant. He's left her. That's why she's got something to moan about. Perhaps they were even married – certainly they were living together. He is to 'leave home no more'.

Back to the beginning. Who assaulted him? She, the wild beast. Not the 'wild beasts' – the old man was again muddling up plural and singular. She was lying in wait for him, somewhere out in the country. She flew at him, raged at him – slaps and scratches. We don't need to be told the result of such an assault. And, of course, she's calling him all the names under the sun. That's 'making her moan' put into prose.

The old man just kept us in touch with the flesh-and-blood experience of the past. For all of us, I say 'Thank you.'

The Come-Home Carol

(Restored)

As I was a-walking in some woodland waste,
There was I set on by a furious wild beast,
She was like a great eagle when someone has come
And has stolen her young one away from his home.

She followed me into a green-growing grove,
To search for that young one whom she did so love,
And when she did find him, oh, how she did cry,
For cold was the harbour where down he did lie.

Then she showed me how warm was her brown, feathered
  nest,
She showed me how soft was her white, downy breast,
She showed me how fountains of milk did outpour,
And she bade me come home, and to leave her no more.

As I was a-walking in some woodland waste,
There was I set on by a furious wild beast,
She was like a great eagle when someone has come
And has stolen her young one away from his home.

The Carnal and the Crane
No. 53, OBC

As I passed by a river-side,
And there as I did rein,
In argument I chanced to hear
A carnal and a crane.

The carnal said unto the crane,
'If all the world should turn,
Before we had the Father,
But now we have the Son.'

'From whence does the Son come?
From where and from what place?'
He said 'In a manger
Between an ox and ass.'

'I pray thee' said the carnal,
'Tell me before thou go,
Was not the mother of Jesus
Conceived by the Holy Ghost?'

'She was the purest virgin
And the cleanest from sin;
She was the handmaid of our Lord
And mother of our King.'

'Where is the golden cradle
That Christ was rocked in?
Where are the silken sheets
That Jesus was wrapt in?'

'A manger was the cradle
That Christ was rocked in;
The provender the asses left
So sweetly he slept on.'

It's lucky I'm carnal, or you'd never have got your folk-carol back!

The beginning is the folk-carol's. There is no Bible story about carnals and cranes. It's adding Bible-story to folk-beginning that has made the broken catechism we have here.

The genuine first six lines will be meaningful if we understand the symbolism of the birds. The crane was the sign outside a brothel (*English Inn Signs* published by Chatto). Why? Because it has a long bill. So the crane, craning forwards, with a long bill, is a man. And we get the 'he' in the third verse.

The carnal? 'The carnal seems to be from the French *"corneille"*, a crow' (OBC). 'She's an old crow.' And carnal is because of the pun I made. Because women love love, always have, always will.

Now we know who the birds are, we can deduce what they are going to say to each other. The woman-symbol and the man-symbol can only discuss woman and man. Their symbolism is limited.

They'll discuss it like the birds they are. The priest didn't want that. He was afraid people might laugh. Real-seeming birds, discussing man and woman's parts in life, will be popular – as in the story Chaucer tells of the cock and hen, debating a family life. The priest, however, wants a new theology so that the carnal and the crane can talk about the Holy Nativity. He altered all the questions and the answers, making the answers roughly fit. We have the beginning of the woman's first question:

If all the world should *turn*
Before we had the ...

He read 'a mother'. But, in its place, he added '... the Father/But now we have the Son'. The carnal, the woman, goes on as she wishes the answer to be,

'From whence does the Son come?
From where and from what place?'

It means her womb. But the Christian answer is another

199

rough fit, for the orthodox answer is surely 'From God'. But the priest has already mentioned God. 'Between an ox and ass' is an unlikely Bible-story happening.

Then she goes on:

> 'I pray thee' said the carnal,
> Tell me before thou go,
> Was not the mother of Jesus
> Conceived by the Holy Ghost?'

She is likely to imagine him going! And well-likely to imagine Jesus, and the awful rhyme of Holy Ghost! He continues:

> 'She was the purest virgin
> And the cleanest from sin;
> She was the handmaid of our Lord
> And mother of our king.'

This, to the carnal! He was relating a hypothetical matter, to a sexual crow!

The carnal challenges:

> 'Where is the golden cradle
> That Christ was rocked in?'

It isn't made of gold. The most absolute desire a mother can have is about the golden cradle which her son, any son, was rocked in, in her womb.

It must have come from a folk-carol, because there is no Bible story, or even legend, that Christ was rocked – and with silken sheets, too! It's the crow, the love-bird again, asking, 'Where is the golden cradle that you, you long-billed man, were rocked in? Didn't it feel like silk?'

Then comes the answer:

> 'A manger was the cradle
> That Christ was rocked in;
> The provender the asses left
> So sweetly he slept on.'

200

The provender must equal the silken sheets!
  Carnal and crane, re-make your carol.

The Crow and the Crane
(Restored)

Man and Woman: As I passed by a river clear,
                  An old crow and a crane
                  In argument I chanced to hear
                  Like woman, and like man.

Woman: The old crow to old thin shanks said,
                  'How did all birds begin?
                  How could there ever be an egg
                  Before there was a hen?'

                  'From where come men?' so she did
                  speak,
                  'From where, and from what place?'
Man: He answered, 'From a crane's long beak
                  Bearing the human race.'

Woman: 'Caw! Caw!' she said. 'Now do not
                  boast,
                  And do not clap your bill.
                  A hen-bird always rules the roost
                  And so she always will.'

Man: 'A chick, when she's a fine, young bird
                  May rule a cock's liking;
                  He'll marry her, as has ocurred,
                  But then becomes her king.'

Woman: 'Who is it has the milken breast
                  All chicks are lain upon?
                  Who is it has the silken nest
                  All cocks do crane upon?'

Man: 'There cannot be a milken breast

201

Till I have lain upon;
There cannot be a silken nest
Till I have craned upon.'

Man and Woman: As I passed by a river clear,
An old crow and a crane
In argument I chanced to hear
Like woman, and like man.

May Carols

Tyrley, Tyrlow
No. 169, OBC

About the field they piped full right,
So merrily the shepherds began to blow;
Adown from heaven they saw a light;
Tyrley, tyrlow, tyrley, tyrlow, tyrley, tyrlow!

Of angels there came a company,
With merry songs and melody,
The shepherds anon 'gan them a-spy;
Tyrley, tyrlow, *etc.*

The shepherds hied them to Bethlem
To see that blessed sunne's beam;
And there they found that glorious stream;
Tyrley, tyrlow, *etc.*

Now pray we to that meke child,
And to his mother that is so mild,
The which was never defiled;
Tyrley, tyrlow, *etc.*

That we may come unto his bliss,
Where joy shall never miss,
Then may we sing in paradise;
Tyrley, tyrlow, *etc.*

I pray you all that be here,
For to sing and make good cheer,
In the worship of God this year;
Tyrley, tyrlow, *etc.*

The shepherds of St Luke (Chapter 2) did not go to Bethlehem to see 'that blessed sunne's beam'. Neither did they pipe. They were keeping watch over their sheep. Also, 'they were sore afraid'. They weren't merry. So these shepherds are not the Biblical ones. Who did get up before dawn to see the sun rise? The lads of the village. And they did pipe and dance so merrily.

Who are these angels who come singing? Not angels, but Angles! They're the girls of the same village, coming to the lads. The 'shepherds' soon spy them!

So here is another May morning song, adapted to Christmas by the reference to Bethlehem. But we've been led up the garden path before. In the next carol, it was to Jerusalem. If we are misled by this one, physical love becomes defilement (see verse 4).

On May morning, everyone knows people danced round the maypole. So that nonsensical 'Tyrley, Tyrlow' was 'Twirl in, Twirl out.' But the priest couldn't leave that, nor translate it into Latin. So he put in nonsense.

Twirl In, Twirl out, Twirl In ...

(Restored)

About the fields lads piped last night
So merrily with all their might,
From a window high they saw a light
Twirl in, twirl out, twirl in ...

Of maids there came a company,
With merry song and minstrelsy,
The lads soon saw that sweet array,
Twirl in, twirl out, twirl in ...

The lads soon led them unto the green
To see the Summer sun's first beam
And there began that glorious game,
Twirl in, twirl out, twirl in ...

And then unto the merry green wood
To pluck the May bough where it stood,
Each lad and lass with heart so good,
Twirl in, twirl out, twirl in ...

And so they came into their bliss
Where we all joy shall never miss,
That we may sing with them in this,
Twirl in, twirl out, twirl in ...

I pray you all that do be here
To do the same, and make good cheer,
In honour of the May this year,
Twirl in, twirl out, twirl in ...

The Bellman's Song

No. 46, OBC

The moon shines bright, and the stars give a light;
A little before it was day,
Our Lord, our God, he called on us,
And bid us awake and pray.

Awake, awake, good people all,
Awake, and you shall hear,
Our Lord, our God, died on the cross
For us whom he loved so dear.

O fair, O fair Jerusalem
When shall I come to thee?
When shall my sorrows have an end
Thy joy that I may see?

The fields were green as green could be,
When from his glorious seat,
Our Lord, our God, he watered us
With his heavenly dew so sweet.

And for the saving of our souls
Christ died upon the cross;
We ne'er shall do for Jesus Christ
As he hath done for us.

The life of man is but a span
And cut down in its flower;
We are here today, and tomorrow are gone,
The creatures of an hour.

Lines from The May Carol
No. 47, OBC

Awake, awake, good people all,
Awake! And you shall hear ...

The early cock so early crows
That is passing the night away ...

A branch of May I have brought to you,
And at your door it stands;
It is but a sprout, but it's well budded-out
By the work of our Lord's hands.

Now my song, that is done, and I must be gone,
No longer can I stay;
So God bless you all, both great and small,
And I wish you a joyful May.

Lines from The May Garland
No. 48, OBC

I've brought you here a bunch of May!
Before your door it stands;
It's well set-out, and well spread about,
By the work of our Lord's hands.

This morning is the first of May,
The primest of the year,
So ladies all, both great and small,
I wish you a joyful cheer.

Lines from As You Like It

This carol they began that hour,
With a hey and a ho and a hey nonino,
How that a life was but a flower,
In the spring time, the only pretty ring time.

[The song begins, 'It was a lover and his lass.]

I have amalgamated three separate carols to make one. First, because of links in their subject-matter. Second, because of their identical form. 'The Bellman's Song' sets the time, 'A little before it was day', which is repeated in 'The May Carol', 'The early cock so early crows.' Then, the 'branch of May I've brought this way' of 'The May Carol' becomes the 'bunch of May/It's well set out, and well spread about' in 'The May Garland'. There are other textual links, like the repetition of 'Awake, awake, good people all' in 'The Bellman's Song' and 'The May Carol'; and the 'I must be gone/No longer can I stay' of the 'Carol' and the 'Garland'.

They have all kept some of the original, complicated verse-form. Not only are all three carols composed in four line verses, of the same line length and rhyme scheme, but they all have the remnants of internal rhymes in the first and third lines. 'The Bellman's Song' begins with such a line – 'The moon shines bright, and the stars give a light' – and has one other, 'The life of man is but a span.' 'The May Carol' has 'It is but a sprout but it's well budded out', 'Now my song, that is done, and I must be gone' and 'So God bless you all, both great and small.' 'The May Day Garland' has 'It's well set out, and well spread about' and 'So ladies all, both great and small'.

There are very few first and third lines which have kept their original form. This shows how much the carols have been altered. The Christian Bible contains no May ceremony. Therefore it has to alter a great deal, to make a May carol fit some Christian occasion. 'The Bellman's Song', for instance, is supposed to be for the Passion, according to the OBC.

However, once we know 'This morning is the first of May',

210

we can fit all the events chronologically together.

We can also see how the Church saddened the songs. For people did not awake on May morning to pray. Nor to hear how Christ died on the cross. Nor to wonder 'When shall my sorrows have an end?' When they sang 'The life of man is but a span', their conclusion was not 'And cut down in its flower' but 'How that a life was but a flower, In the spring time, the only pretty ring time'. 'Let's get married at once!' (or as good as), said the original carol. How we've been hoodwinked by those who wore hoods.

The May Day Carol

(Restored)

A branch of May I've brought this way
And at your door it stands,
It is but a sprout but it's well budded-out,
It will bloom in all your lands!

Awake, awake, for that bough's sake,
Awake and you shall see
How fair they make, both bush and brake,
How fair is the tall May Tree.

The moon shone bright, and the stars gave light,
A little 'fore it was day,
The cock was right, the dawn in sight,
He could crow the night away.

The fields were green, as has ever been seen,
When we went to the wood,
We sought the limb that's ever been
The spring sign of our good.

And for our comfort, for our sport,
The May has sprung at once,
Then let us court in that same sort
As the tree has done for us.

The life of man is but a span
It blossoms like a flower,
Then let us plan while love we can
To welcome in this hour.

This morning is of May the first,
The youngest of the year,
So all ladies, I wish you this,
The best of joyful cheer.

A branch of May I've brought this way
And at your door it stands,
It is but a sprout but it's well budded-out,
It will bloom in all your lands!

Further Reading

Further Reading

Bowra, C.M., *Primitive Song* (Weidenfeld & Nicolson, 1962)

(ed.) Dearmer, Percy, R. Vaughan Williams and Martin Shaw, *The Oxford Book of Carols* (Oxford University Press, 1928)

Greene, R., *The Early English Carols* (Oxford University Press, 1977)

Harrison, Michael, *The Roots of Witchcraft* (Muller, 1973)

Larkin, Philip, *High Windows* (Faber & Faber, 1974)

Larwood and Hotton, *English Inn Signs* (Blaketon Hall, 1985)

Magnusson, M., *Vikings. Hammer of the North* (Orbis, 1986)

Opie, Peter and Iona, *The Oxford Dictionary of Nursery Rhymes* (Oxford University Press, 1952)

(ed.) Opie, Peter and Iona, *The Puffin Book of Nursery Rhymes* (Puffin, 1963)

Partridge, Eric, *Dictionary of Historical Slang* (Penguin, 1972). Abridged by Jacqueline Simpson, 1972

(ed.) Rawson, Philip, *Primitive Erotic Art* (Weidenfeld & Nicolson, 1973)

Renoir, Jean, *Renoir: My Father* (Collins, 1962)

Routley, Eric, *The English Carol* (Herbert Jenkins, 1958)

Rye, W., *Songs of Norfolk* (1897)

(ed.) Sharp, Cecil, *English Country Folk Songs* (Novello & Co., reprinted 1961)

Sharp, Cecil, *Folk Songs Collected in the Appalachian Mountains* (1917)

Walsh, I., *Twenty-Four New Country Dances* (Kidson, 1708)

Watson, William, *The Newcastle Song Book* (1842)

Index

Index of First Lines